Derech Hashem

The Way of the God

Kabbalist Rabbi
Moshe Chaim Luzzatto

The Ra'MHaL

There is no known book without mistakes. Therefore, I ask in every language of application if anyone has any questions, comments, clarifications, corrections, please send to:

simchatchaim@yahoo.com

All material used in this section may not be used for commercial purposes, but only for study and teaching.

To get this book or books and information Email me at:

simchatchaim@yahoo.com

Copyright©All Rights Reserved to

www.simchatchaim.com

YB"S©All rights reserved to the Editor

First Edition 2023

TABLE OF CONTENTS

3	Rabbi Moshe Chaim Luzzatto
7	Introduction to the book from the Rabbi

Part One

11	On the Creator
14	On the Purpose of Creation
18	On Mankind
29	On Human Responsibility
38	On the Spiritual Realm

Part Two

47	On Divine Providence in General
49	On Mankind in This World
57	On Personal Providence
72	On Israel and the Nations
80	On How Providence Works
84	On the System of Providence
88	On the Influence of the Stars
90	On Specific Modes of Providence

Part Three

97	On the Soul and Its Activities
102	On Divine Names and Witchcraft
113	On Divine Inspiration and Prophecy
117	On the Prophetic Experience
128	On Moshe's Unique Status

Part Four

135	On Divine Service
136	On Torah Study
142	On Love and Fear of God

Derech   TABLE OF CONTENTS   Hashem

143	On the Sh'ma and Its Blessings
160	On Prayer
163	On the Daily Order of Prayer
178	On Divine Service and the Calendar
183	On Seasonal Commandments
198	On Blessings

Moshe Chaim Luzzatto

Moshe Chaim Luzzatto (Ramchal) was an Italian rabbi, kabbalist and philosopher who also wrote dramatic works and literary criticism. Gifted with an almost photographic memory, he wrote many works, some which became standards of kabbalah and ethics. He was suspected of Sabbateanism, but was exonerated by his teachers and colleagues with a warning to cease engaging in speculative kabbalistic writing. Toward the end of his life he moved to the Land of Israel.

Early life

Moshe Chaim Luzzatto was born in 1707 in the Jewish Ghetto of Padua, Italy. The son of Jacob Vita and Diamente Luzzatto, he received classical Jewish and Italian education, showing a predilection for literature at a very early age. He may have attended the University of Padua and certainly associated with a group of students there, known to dabble in mysticism and alchemy. With his vast knowledge in religious lore, the arts, and science, he quickly became the dominant figure in that group. His writings demonstrate mastery of the Tanakh, the Talmud, and the rabbinical commentaries and codes of Jewish law.

Poetry and literature

At an early age, he began a thorough study of the Hebrew language and of poetic composition. He wrote epithalamia and elegies, a noteworthy example of the latter being the dirge on the death of his teacher Cantarini, a lofty poem of twenty-four verses written in classical Hebrew. Before age 20, he had begun his composition of 150 hymns modeled on the Biblical Psalter. In these psalms, composed in conformity with the laws of parallelism, he freed himself from all foreign influences, imitating the style of the Bible so faithfully that his poems seem entirely a renaissance of Biblical words and thoughts. They provoked the criticism of the Rabbis, however, and were one of the causes of the persecutions to which Luzzatto was later subjected. R. Jacob Poppers of Frankfort-on-the-Main thought it unpardonable presumption to attempt to equal the "anointed of the God of Jacob." Only two psalms are known of which it can with certainty be said that they belonged to Luzzatto's psalter; in addition seven hymns by him which were sung at the inauguration of the enlarged Spanish synagogue at Padua appeared in the work "Ḥanukkat ha-Maron" (Venice, 1729); but it is not certain whether they were taken from the psalter.

As a youth Luzzatto essayed also dramatic poetry, writing at the age of 17 his first Biblical drama, "Shimshon u-Felistim," (of which only fragments have been preserved, in another work of his). This youthful production foreshadows the coming master; it is perfect in versification, simple in language, original and thoughtful in substance. This first large work was followed by the "Leshon Limmudim," a discussion of Hebrew style with a new theory of Hebrew versification, in which the author showed his thorough knowledge of classical rhetoric. It is in a certain sense a scientific demonstration of the neoclassic Italian style, in contrast with the medieval. There is a vast difference between Luzzatto's style, which recalls the simplicity, smoothness, and vigor of the Bible, and the insipid, exaggerated, and affected work of his contemporaries. The book, dedicated to his teacher Bassani, was printed at Mantua 1727, with a text which deviates from the manuscript formerly in the possession of M. S. Ghirondi.

In the same year or somewhat later, Luzzatto wrote his allegorical festival drama "Migdal 'Oz" (or "Tummat Yesharim"), on the occasion of the marriage of his friend Israel Benjamin Bassani. This four-act play, which shows Latin and Italian as well as Biblical influence, illustrates the victory of justice over iniquity. It is masterly in versification and melodious in language, the lyrical passages being especially lofty; and it has a wealth of pleasing imagery reminiscent of Guarini's "Pastor Fido." The drama was edited by M. Letteris, and published with notes by S. D. Luzzatto and prolegomena by Franz Delitzsch, Leipsic, 1837.

Controversy
The turning point in Luzzatto's life came at the age of twenty, when he claimed to have received direct instruction from an angel (known as a maggid). While stories of such encounters with celestial entities were not unknown in kabbalistic circles, it was unheard of for someone of such a young age. His peers were enthralled by his written accounts of these "Divine lessons", but the leading Italian rabbinical authorities were highly suspicious and threatened to excommunicate him. Just one hundred years earlier another young mystic, Shabbatai Zvi (1626–1676),

had rocked the Jewish world by claiming to be the Messiah. Although, at one point, Zvi had convinced many European and Middle Eastern rabbis of his claim, the episode ended with him recanting and converting to Islam. The global Jewish community was still reeling from that, and the similarities between Luzzatto's writings and Zvi's were perceived as being particularly dangerous and heretical.

These writings, only some of which have survived, are often misunderstood to describe a belief that the Ramchal and his followers were key figures in a messianic drama that was about to take place. In this contentious interpretation, he identified one of his followers as the Messiah, son of David, and assumed for himself the role of Moses, claiming that he was that biblical figure's reincarnation.

Departure from Italy

After threats of excommunication and many arguments, Luzzatto finally came to an understanding with the leading Italian rabbis, including his decision not to write the maggid's lessons or teach mysticism. In 1735, Luzzatto left Italy for Amsterdam, believing that in the more liberal environment there, he would be able to pursue his mystical interests. Passing through Germany, he appealed to the local rabbinical authorities to protect him from the threats of the Italian rabbis. They refused and forced him to sign a document stating that all the teachings of the maggid were false.

Amsterdam

When Luzzatto finally reached Amsterdam, he was able to pursue his Kabbalah studies relatively unhindered. Earning a living as a diamond cutter, he continued writing but refused to teach. It was in this period that he wrote his magnum opus the Mesillat Yesharim (1740), essentially an ethical treatise but with certain mystical underpinnings. The book presents a step-by-step process by which every person can overcome the inclination to sin and might eventually experience a divine inspiration similar to prophecy. Another prominent work, Derekh Hashem (The Way of God) is a concise work on the core theology of Judaism. The same concepts are discussed in brief in a smaller book called Maamar Halkarim (the English translation of this book is now available on the Web with the title "Essay on Fundamentals"). Da'at Tevunot ("The Knowing Heart") also found its existence in Amsterdam as the missing link between rationality and Kabbalah, a dialogue between the intellect and the soul. On the other hand, Derech Tevunot ("The Way of Understanding") introduces the logic which structures Talmudic debates as a means to understanding the world.

One major rabbinic contemporary who praised Luzzatto's writing was Rabbi Eliyahu of Vilna, the Vilna Gaon (1720–1797), who was considered to be the most authoritative Torah sage of the modern era as well as a great kabbalist himself. He was reputed to have said after reading the Mesillat Yesharim, that were Luzzatto still alive, he would have walked from Vilna to learn at Luzzatto's feet. He stated that having read the work, the first ten chapters contained not a superfluous word.

Luzzatto also wrote poetry and drama. Although most of it is seemingly secular, some scholars claim to have identified mystical undertones in this body of work as well. His writing is strongly influenced by the Jewish poets of Spain and by contemporary Italian authors.

The cantor of the Sephardic synagogue in Amsterdam, Abraham Caceres, worked with Luzzatto to set several of his poems to music.

Acre, Israel
Frustrated by his inability to teach kabbalah, Luzzatto left Amsterdam for the Holy Land in 1743, settling in Acre. Three years later, he and his family died in a plague.

Legacy
Though it is accepted by scholars that his tomb is in Kafr Yasif, where some assume to have identified it, his burial place is traditionally said to be near the Talmudic sage Rabbi Akiva in Tiberias, northern Israel. It is noteworthy that there are many scholars who make some comparison between the Ramchal and Rabbi Akiva. Some believe that the Ramchal is actually a Gilgul (reincarnation) of Rabbi Akiva. Probably also because Kafr Yasif is now an Arab town while Tiberias is Jewish, the Tiberias tomb is the destination of almost all of the pilgrims seeking his final resting place.

Derech Hashem

Introduction

[When one approaches a subject] the most effective way to apprehend it is to break down all its details, categorize them, and discern their interrelationships.

And so, based on its place will be the examinations by which it is necessary to examine it, according to its nature, to fully understand its form and its function: If it is a part, he will seek to know the whole of which it is a part. If it is a specific, he will seek to analyze the category. If it is a cause, he will seek to analyze its effects; if an effect, its cause. If it is an association, he will seek [knowledge] about the subject, as well as to know what type of association it is - if precedent, if antecedent or if accompanying; if essential or contingent; and if potential or actual. All of these are examinations without which he will not completely comprehend the form of the thing. With all of it [However,], he may contemplate the nature of the thing, to know if it is constant or limited. And if it is limited, he should investigate its limits. For surely any true matter will end up becoming false if it is ascribed to a subject not fitting it or if it is seen outside of its limits.

However, one must consider that the number of details is much too great for the intellect of man to contain, and it is impossible for one to know them all. Yet what is fit is for him to attempt to know the general principles. As the nature of every principle is to contain [knowledge about] many details. So, when one grasps one principle, he [also] grasps a great number of details. And even though he has not yet examined them because they are [only] details [subsumed by] the principle; [nevertheless] when one of them comes to him, he is not stunted by knowing it, since [its] general matter - which perforce must exist - is already known to him. And likewise, the Sages, may their memory be blessed, said (Sifrei Devarim 306:20), "Matters of Torah should always be in your hands as general principles and not as details."

Yet what is required in the knowledge of general principles is knowing them through all of their limits and in all of their characteristics, as I wrote above. And you must even pay attention to, and not neglect, things that first appear to be lacking any application. For there is no small or large thing in a general principle that does not have [some] application in the details. And if it does not add or take away anything about some of the details, it will certainly have great application about others. Since a principle is a principle about all the details, it must contain [some information] about each of them. Hence you must be very exacting about this and examine their functions, their relationships and their connections with great precision. And you must examine their processes and progression very well - [to know] how one matter leads to another, from the beginning to the end. 'And then you will be successful and then you will understand.'

Derech   Introduction   Hashem

Now see, pleasant reader, that it is according to these things that I have written this short composition. And my intention in it was to present with clarity in front of you the general principles of faith and [divine] service in such a way that you could understand them properly, so, that they create a model for you sufficiently free of jumble and confusion. Then you will clearly see their roots and branches and contexts; such that they will sit well upon your heart, and you will acquire them with your mind in the most superior way. And from then on, it will be easy for you to find knowledge of God in all of the sections of the Torah and its commentaries and to understand all of its secrets, 'according to the blessing that the Lord, your God, will bestow upon you.' And see that I have tried to arrange the things in an order that I have thought to be more pleasant, and with words that I have considered fitting, in order to give a full picture of these things which I have decided to teach you. Hence you must now also, be precise about all this and hold on to it with outstanding diligence until you find a place where it will help you. And do not neglect any nuance, lest an essential matter escape you. Rather this is what you should do: Be precise with all the words, and make efforts to understand the content of all of the matters and to store all of their truth in your mind. Then you will find it to be a comfort that will benefit you. And behold I have entitled the book, The Way of God. For it truly consists of His ways, may He be blessed, that He revealed to us through His prophets and made known to us through His Torah, and by which He leads us and leads all of His creatures. And I have divided it into four sections: In the first I will speak about the principle of the foundations of existence and its details; in the second about His providence, may He be blessed; in the third about prophecy; and in the fourth about [divine] service. And you, my brother [among] all the seekers of the Lord - go in this 'way' and may the Lord be with you and give you eyes to see and ears to hear the 'wonders of His Torah.' Amen, may it be His will.

Part One

On the Creator

The Existence of G-d: Every Jew needs to believe and know that a First Being exists. [This Being] is without beginning or end. He brought into existence and [constantly] creates everything that is present in existence. This [Being] is G-d.

Additionally [every Jew] needs to know that the essential reality of this Being, G-d, cannot be [adequately] grasped by any [created being] at all. The only thing known about Him is that He is totally Perfect, having no deficiencies at all. This information, However, is only known through a tradition received from our ancestors and the prophets [we couldn't conclude it on our own].

The necessity of His existence: One also, must know that the existence of this Being, may His name be blessed, is a necessary existence, the absence of which is completely impossible.

His being independent of another: One must also, know that His existence, may He be blessed, is not dependent at all on anything besides Him. Rather His existence is independently necessary.

His simplicity: And likewise, he must know that His existence, may He be blessed, is a simple (undifferentiated) existence without composition or multiplicity at all. And all of the perfections are found within Him in a simple way. The explanation of this is [as follows]: Many different capabilities are found within the soul, each one of which has its own domain: By way of example, memory is one capability, willpower is another capability and imagination is [yet] another capability. And not one of these enters the domain of its fellow at all, as surely the domain of memory is one domain and the domain of willpower is another domain. And willpower does not enter into the domain of memory, nor does memory [enter] into the domain of willpower. And so, [too] with all of them. However, the Master, may His name be blessed, does not have different capabilities, even though He actually has properties that are differing within us. For surely He is willful and is wise and is powerful and He is perfect in every perfection; However, the truth of His existence is one matter that includes within His truth and domain (meaning the truth of His being, as having a domain is not applicable to Him, may He be blessed - rather it is only by way of literary license) everything that is a perfection. And it comes out that He has all of the perfections - not as an addition to His essence and the truth of His being, but rather from the angle of the truth of His being itself, which includes in its truth all of the perfections in its truth; [as it] would be impossible for this [type of] being without all of the perfections, from the angle of itself. And this approach is truly very far from our comprehension and our perception.

And it is almost as if we have no way to elucidate it or words to explain it. For our perceptions and imaginations only grasp things limited by [their] nature which is created by Him, may He be blessed - as this perception is what our senses perceive and bring to the mind. And with the creatures, [these capabilities] are surely many and differing matters. However, we have already prefaced that the truth of His existence, may He be blessed, is not grasped and it cannot be compared to what we see with the creatures. For their properties and existences are not at all the same, such that we could learn one from the other. However, this is also, from the things that are known through the tradition, but they are validated by investigation through nature itself, with its axioms and properties. For it is impossible that there nevertheless not exist a Being removed from all nature, axioms and limits, from all lack and deficiency, from all multiplicity and composition, from all relationship and value and from the contingency of the creatures - to be the Ultimate Cause for all that exists and for all that develops from it. For without this Existence, those things that we see existing and their continuation would be impossible.

His Unity: And it is also, required for one to know that it is necessary for this Being, may His name be blessed, to be one and not more. The explanation of this is that it is impossible for there to exist many beings the existence of which is independently necessary. Rather this necessary and perfect Existence must be only one. And if there exist other beings, they only exist because He made them exist with His will; so, it comes out that they are all dependent on Him, and not existing from themselves.

It comes out that the sum of these root principles are six. And they are: The truth of His existence, may He be blessed; His perfection; the necessity of His existence; His being independent of anything besides Him; His simplicity; and His Unity.

On the Purpose of Creation

The purpose of creation: See that the purpose of creation was to give from His goodness, may He be blessed, to another besides Him. And behold, see that His alone is true perfection, devoid of all deficiencies. And there is no other perfection like it at all. So, it comes out that any perfection that resembles [it] - besides His perfection, may He be blessed - is not true perfection. Rather it is called perfection relative to something more deficient than it. But complete perfection is only His perfection, may He be blessed. And therefore, since His desire, may He be blessed, was to do good to others, it would not be sufficient for Him to do a little good, but rather [only] in giving the full goodness that is possible for the creatures to receive. And in His alone, may He be blessed, being the true good, His good desire would only be satisfied by giving others that very good that is within Him, may He be blessed, from the angle of Himself - which is the truly perfect good. Yet surely from another angle, this good is impossible to be found anywhere but in Him. Therefore, His wisdom decreed that the nature of this true giving would be that a place be given to the creatures to cleave to Him, may He be blessed, according to the measure of what is possible for them to cleave. And so, it comes out that what would be impossible from the angle of themselves - that they would be described by the same perfection as His perfection, may He be blessed - nevertheless surely comes to them according to the measure that it is possible for them to be described by His perfection, may He be blessed, from the angle of their cleaving to Him. And it comes out that they benefit from this true good, relative to that which is possible for them to benefit from it. [Likewise,,] it comes out that His intention, may His name be blessed, in the creation that He created was to create someone that can benefit from His goodness, may He be blessed, in the manner that it is possible for him to benefit from it.

The nature of perfection, deficiencies and the acquisition of perfection: However, His wisdom decreed that in that this good is perfect, it is fitting that the one who benefits from it, own that good - [meaning] one that acquires the good himself and not one that has the good joined to him in a contingent way. And see that this is called a little resemblance - in the measure that it is possible - to His perfection, may He be blessed. For surely, He, may His name be blessed, is perfect from Himself, and not contingently so. Rather from the angle of the truth of His nature, He is required to have that perfection. And He is necessarily devoid of deficiencies. However, it is impossible that this be found in anyone besides Him - that his truth requires him to have this perfection and be devoid of deficiencies. Yet to resemble it a little, it is required that it at least acquire the perfection that the truth of its nature does not require and remove the deficiencies that were possible in it. Therefore He decreed and arranged that the matters of perfection and the matters of deficiency be created; and a creature be created that would have the equal possibility of both of these matters; and that mechanisms be given to this creature through which it could acquire the perfections for itself and remove the deficiencies from itself. And then it would happen that it would become similar to its Creator, in that which is possible for it; and it would be fitting to cleave to Him and to benefit from His goodness.

However, besides this creature that acquired perfection being fit to cleave to his Creator, may He be blessed, from the angle of its resembling Him - see, that by its acquisition of perfection for itself, it comes out that it increases its clinging to Him, until the end of its acquisition of perfection and its cleaving to Him all become one thing. For in that His existence, may He be blessed, is the true perfection, as we have written; anything that is perfect only relates to Him, like a branch to the root. As even if it does not reach the root perfection, it is a continuation and an outgrowth of it. And behold that any true perfection is surely His existence, may He be blessed; and any deficiency is only the absence of His goodness, may He be blessed, and the hiding of His face. So, it comes out that the shining of His face, may He be blessed, and His closeness are the root and the cause of all perfection that will be; and the hiding of His face is the root and the cause of all the deficiency - such that according to the measure of the hiding, is the measure of the deficiency that results from it. Therefore when this creature - that stands evenly between the perfections and the deficiencies that are outgrowths of the shining and the hiding - strengthens itself with perfections and acquires them for itself on its own; behold, it attaches [itself] to Him, may He be blessed, who is their root and their source. And according to that which it increases perfection, so, does it increase in attachment to Him; until when it reaches the end of the acquisition of perfection, behold it reaches the end of attachment and cleaving to Him, may He be blessed. So, it benefits from His good and perfects itself in Him and becomes, itself, the owner of its good and its perfection.

The main creature and the secondary ones: And see that given that these different things of perfection and deficiency that we mentioned are in existence and that the creature that we mentioned has the characteristic that is necessary - [meaning,] the possibility for the two things and the ability to [access] them, such that it may acquire perfection and remove deficiencies - and that it has the mechanisms for this thing - [meaning,] to acquire this perfection: There are certainly many different components required in the creation and many relationships between these components before it can be successful in the purpose set for it.

Nevertheless, the creature that was envisioned for this great thing - meaning, to cleave to Him, may He be blessed, as I have written - is the one called the essence of all creation. And everything else that is found in existence is only to help in a certain way or a certain characteristic, for this purpose to be successful and to come about. Therefore, they are called secondary to the main creature that we have mentioned.

Of course, the main creature is truly the human specie. And all of the other creatures - whether taller than he or lower than he - are only for his sake to fulfill his function due to all of the many and different characteristics that are fitting to be found in them, and as I will write about in the continuation, with God's help (Part 4, On Blessings 1-2). And see that education and all of the proper traits are mechanisms for perfection that are found for a man to perfect himself; and physical matters and bad traits are the mechanisms for deficiency - that we have mentioned - among which man is placed, for him to acquire perfection.

On Mankind

As we have discussed, humanity is the creature created for the purpose of drawing close to God. They are placed between perfection and deficiency, and it is in their hands to earn perfection. Humanity must earn this perfection, However, through their own desire and choice because if they were forced to choose perfection then they would not actually be its master, and God's purpose would not be fulfilled. It as therefore necessary to create humanity with free will. One's inclinations are therefore balanced between good and evil and they are not compelled toward either. They have the power of choice, able to choose either side knowingly and willingly, as well as to possess whichever one they wish. Humanity was therefore created with both a good urge and an evil urge. They have the power to incline in whichever direction they choose.

The joining of the body and the soul: However, in order for this matter to be accomplished appropriately, the Supreme Wisdom decreed that man be composed of two opposites - meaning to say, from a spiritual and pure soul and from an earthly body. And since each one of them naturally inclines to its side - meaning to say, the body towards physicality and the soul towards spirituality - it comes out that there is a war between them in such a way that if the soul wins, it will raise the body with it; but if man allows the physical to win in him, the body will surely be lowered and the soul will be lowered with it. And that man will not be fit for perfection, and will be pushed away from it, God forbid. But that man [still] has the ability to humble his physical [side] before his spiritual [side] and soul and acquire his perfection, as I have written.

This world and the next world: However, His Goodness, may He be blessed, decreed that there be a limit to this striving that is required for a person to acquire perfection and that when he finishes his striving, he obtains his [level of] perfection and is left with his enjoyment for ever and ever. Therefore, two time periods were designed for him - one is the time for work and one is the time for receiving the reward. However, the [divine] attribute of good is greater, such that the work has a [limited] time, as His Wisdom, may He be blessed, decreed be appropriate for it. But there is no end to the receiving of reward. Rather one delights and continues with the perfection that he acquired for himself for ever and ever.

The change in man's conditions with the change of time periods: However, according to the change in the time period, so, is it fit that his condition and his other circumstances change. For in all of the time of striving, he surely needs to be in a situation in which all the things that he needs for this process of striving can be found. The explanation of this is that it is surely necessary that the war that we mentioned between the spiritual and the material be present for him. And there should not be anything for him to impede the material from ruling and doing its [function], according to the measure that is fitting for it. And there should be nothing impeding the spirit from ruling, as is fitting for it, and doing its [function]. Likewise, there should not be anything that would cause the material to be strengthened more than is fitting, and also, [nothing] causing the spirit to be strengthened more than is fitting. For even though from one angle, [the latter] would have appeared to be better; behold according to the true intention and the desired matter about man - which is the acquisition of perfection through his striving - it is not good. But at the time of receiving the reward, it is surely fitting that the situation be the opposite of this. For behold, all that the material would rule at that time was surely only to darken [man's awareness] and prevent the soul from cleaving to the Creator, may He be blessed. Therefore, at that time, it is appropriate for only the soul rule; and that the material be completely drawn after it in such a way that it not be impeded by it at all. And indeed, two worlds were therefore created - this world and the next world. The place and the natural conditions of this world are what is fitting for man all the time of his striving. And the place and the natural conditions of the next world are what is fitting for him at the time of receiving the reward.

The human specie changed: And among that which one must also, know is that the nature of the human specie that we see and distinguish now is not like at first. Rather there was a great change in him, and that is the matter of the sin of the first man (Adam) - as through it, man and the world were changed from what they were at the beginning. And there are indeed many components of this change and its outgrowths, and we will write about them in the continuation with God's help (Part 2, On Israel and the Nations 2). And it comes out that discussion about the human specie and distinguishing its properties [needs to be] doubled. For he and his properties before the sin will be discussed, as will he and his properties from the aspect of [the situation] after the sin - as we shall still elucidate, with God's help (Below, Paragraph 8).

Behold that at the time of his formation, the first man was completely in the situation that we have mentioned until now. This means that he was surely joined from the two opposite parts that we mentioned - which are the soul and the body. And there were the two [possibilities] in the world - the good and the evil, and he stood between them evenly, to cleave to the one of them that he would want. And it was surely fitting for him to choose the good, that his soul should win over his body and his spirit over his materiality; and then he would have been perfected immediately and stayed in his perfection forever.

The effects of the soul on the body: And you need to know that even thought we don't feel any effect of the soul on the body except for life and awareness, behold that among its axioms is that it purifies the actual body and its material, and it raises it up - one lift after [another] - with regard to its becoming fit to accompany it in the pleasure [of] perfection. And in truth, the first man would have reached this thing if he had not sinned - his soul would have purified his body, one purification after [another], until it would have been purified [with] the necessary and established measure for everlasting delight.

The outgrowths of the sin of the first man: But once he sinned, a great change happened to things. And that is that at first there were surely sufficient deficiencies in the creation that the first man would be in the equal condition that we mentioned, so, there would be room for him to earn perfections through the 'effort of his [own] hands.' With his sin, However, deficiencies were added; and they grew in the essence of man and in all of the entire creation. Moreover, the redress became more difficult than before. The explanation of this is that surely at the beginning it was easy for [man] to go away from the deficiency planted in him and to acquire perfection. For the Supreme Wisdom set up the things like this according to the traits of good and fairness. And since man was not the cause of the evil and the deficiency within him - but it was rather planted in him in his creation - when he removed himself from the evil and turned to the good, he was surely immediately able to go away from deficiency and acquire perfection. However, with his sin - since it was through him that perfection became more hidden than it was and the deficiencies grew, and he was the one that caused evil to himself - it would no longer be as easy for him to return and to go away from deficiency and acquire perfection as it was at the time that he was not the cause of his deficiency, but was rather [just] created like that from his beginning, as I have written. All the more so, [would it be harder], as the striving required of him now to reach perfection would perforce be doubled: For he would first need that man and the world return to the condition that existed at the beginning before the sin; and then afterwards to rise above that condition to a condition of perfection to which it was fit for man to rise.

Death and resurrection: However, besides all of this, His trait of [strict] judgement, may He be blessed, decreed that from now on, man and the world could not reach perfection so, long as they are in a corrupted state - meaning, the form they have now, in which evil grew. Rather they perforce need a transformation beyond the perdition - meaning, death for man and destruction for all of the other things in existence that became corrupted with him. And the soul can [no longer] purify the body until after it first goes out of it and the body dies and decomposes. And then [the body] returns and is built [as] a new structure, and the soul enters it and purifies it. And likewise, the whole world will become destroyed from its current form, and it will return and be built in a different form that is fitting for perfection. And therefore, it was decreed upon man that he die, and [then] come back and live [again]. And this is the matter of the revival of the dead. And [it was decreed] about the world that it will be destroyed and [then] come back and be renewed - and this is the matter that they, may their memory be blessed, said (Sanhedrin 97a), "The world will [exist] for six thousand years, and be destroyed for one [thousand]; but at the end of a thousand years, the Holy One, blessed be He, returns and renews the world.

And behold according to this root concept, the time of the true repayment - meaning the time of receiving the reward, that we mentioned above - and its place, is after the resurrection in the world that will be renewed. And man will enjoy it with his body and his soul, in that his body will be purified by the soul and prepared by it to enjoy that good. Yet people will be distinguished and their levels and positions will differ, according to the measure of that which they toiled in the world of work, and according to that [which] they strove to access perfection. For the soul will shine according to this measure, and light up the body and purify it. And both of them will acquire preciousness and stature and be fitting to approach the Master, blessed be He, to be lit by the light of His countenance and to enjoy His true good.

The world of souls: And yet since death was decreed upon man - and as I have written - and it comes out that this combination needs to divide for some time and come back to join; behold it is fitting that there also, be at this time of division an appropriate place for these two divided parts, for that which is desired for this [period of] division. And see that the body needs to return to its element and separate [from] its combination and lose its form. And since it was dirt, it must return to it - and this is what He, may His name be blessed, said to Adam, "As you are dirt and to the dirt you shall return" (Genesis 3:19). But the soul (that has merited reward through its deeds) surely only has to wait until that which needs to be done to the body is done - meaning the de-solidifying and decomposition of the first [body] and its remaining in the dirt all the time it needs, and its formation anew afterwards, when [the soul] returns to enter it. However, it needs a place between this and that. And, in truth, it is for this reason that the world of souls was established - that the meritorious souls enter it, after their leaving the body, and dwell there in a restful place all the time that the matters that are fitting to happen to the body happen to it. And see that all of that time, these souls will dwell in loftiness and delight, similar to that which will be given to them afterwards at the time of the true repayment that we mentioned above. For his loftiness in the world of souls will also, certainly be measured according to the actions that he has done, according to which his repayment afterwards at that time will also, be measured. But the true perfection destined for those who merit it will not be attained - not by the body and not by the soul - until their joining together a second time, after the resurrection.

The purpose of man in the world of souls: However, besides the world of souls being a place for the souls to dwell and wait for the body - as we have said - behold there is also, another great purpose found in it for the souls themselves, and afterwards for the body for what it needs afterwards at the time of the resurrection. And that is that after there was the decree on man, that he could only reach his perfection after death - even though it is already apparent about him from the angle of his deeds while he is still alive (as without this, it would never be coming to him; as the time of acquiring perfection is surely only in this world, before he dies, as we have written) - another extension of this decree is that all the time that it is in the body in this world, to which evil cleaves [and] from which it is impossible to completely separate, it too will be darkened and hazy. And even though through the good deeds that a person does, [the soul] acquires precious perfection for itself, the thing cannot be revealed; and it cannot shine with the splendor that would have been fit for it to shine according to that preciousness that it would have truly reached. Rather it all stays suppressed in itself until the time that is given for it to be revealed. However, the delay is not from its side at all, but rather from the side of the body, as we have written. And [the body] itself loses in this; in that during all of that time, it does not receive the purification that would be fitting that it receives, as we have written. Nevertheless, [the soul] also, loses, in that it is suppressed inside itself and is not able to express its splendor. Moreover, it does not perform the act that is fit for it, which is the purification of the body. And if it did perform it, it would perfect itself greatly from the angle of the essence of this act itself. For it is surely a perfect act - to do good to, and perfect, another. And also, this act is the act that is appropriate for it according to its nature and its axiom - as it was created for this. And every creature is perfected when it does that which it was designed to do by its Creator, may He be blessed; and it is lacking perfection all the time that it does not do it. However, when the soul leaves the body and goes to the world of souls, it surely expresses itself there and shines its splendor according to that which is fitting according to it deeds. And that which it can attain there, all the time that it is there, strengthens it from all that it was weakened in the body, and it becomes more equipped to that which is fitting for it to do at the time of the resurrection - until, when it does return to the body at the fitting time, it will be able to perform the act appropriate for it, meaning the purification that we mentioned.

The difference between the entry of the soul into the embryo and its entry [into the body at the time of] the resurrection: However, you need to know that even now, when the soul enters the body of the fetus - even though it has not yet acquired perfection through its deeds - surely from the angle of its internal preciousness and splendor, it would have been fitting that it give its great purification to the material [body] to the point that it would go away from being of the human specie. Nevertheless, His decree, may He be blessed, suppresses it and hides its power and reduces its splendor in such a way that this matter not come out from it. Rather it dwells there concealed in itself, according to that measure that is required according to the Highest Intention. And so, it operates in the body according to that arrangement and measure that is required from His Wisdom, may He be blessed. And behold [likewise,] according to its good deeds that it continuously does; it should have expressed itself and shined, as we have said, and then its purification would have reached the body. However, according to the decree that we explained above, it is not possible for it [to do so] until it is in the world of souls. Nevertheless, when it returns to the body after the resurrection, it will not reduce itself nor hide, but rather enter [the body] with all of its splendor and all of its power. And then it will immediately purify the body [with] a great purification and it will not need a graduated growth, [as] is needed for children right now. Rather it will immediately make it shine at that time, and it will will immediately purify it [with] a great purification. However, this will not prevent the body and the soul together from having elevations and more elevations [at that time]. Rather the point is that immediately with the entry of the soul into the body, that man will be precious and elevated and his body will immediately receive [its] first purification. [And] it will be more elevated than all that it was during all the days of its first life. And that purification will be according to all of the good deeds that he already did. And they put him on a level that is appropriate for him, and he will be among those that merit to enjoy perfection. And afterwards, they will both be lifted by elevations and more elevations, according to that which is fitting for one who is on that [particular] level.

On Human Responsibility

Regarding the condition of man in this world, two matters will be examined: Man's own disposition in his parts and their combination; and the place in which he is put in all that concerns him.

Man's disposition in this world: Regarding the examination of man himself, we have already mentioned how he is composite, [being] composed of two opposites - meaning the soul and the body. However, we see with our eyes that his materiality is dominant and that its effects upon him are very strong. For immediately after his birth, he is almost all material and the intellect barely act within him. Then as he grows up, the intellect strengthens and grows in each person according to his specifications. Nevertheless [his] materiality does not cease ruling over him and directing him towards its interests. Yet if he grows in his wisdom, he studies it and strengthens himself in its paths - he will surely exert himself to conquer his nature and never release the bridle of his desires from his hand; and to push himself to go in the ways of the intellect. The center of these matters is that we see that in the existence of matter and its [physical] reality, there is turbidity and darkness in its nature. And that is a reality very far [from] - and [even] the opposite of - what is the true [path] for those coming near to God, may He be blessed, and cleaving to His holiness. And even though the soul is, in itself, pure and elevated - see that when it enters the material body and becomes intertwined with it, it becomes divorced and pushed away from its natural concern to a concern that is its opposite, and [then] becomes suppressed within it by force. It cannot leave this unless it pushes with a a stronger power than the compelling force. And since the Master, may He be blessed, decreed that this composition of man's body and his soul can never be separated, (the explanation of this is that the separation of death is only something temporary until the revival of the dead; However, afterwards it needs to return to the body, and [then] both of them will exist together for ever and ever) behold it is required that the soul make efforts and strengthen itself, and continually weaken the power of the darkness of materiality until the body remains without darkness. And then [the body] may rise up with it to be enlightened by the light of the Most High - in contrast to the [soul's] having been darkened and lowered with [the body] at first. However, man in this world is in a condition wherein the material is strong, as we have written. And since the material is turbid and dark, man finds himself in great darkness and far from that which it is appropriate for him to be, which is to be cleaving to Him, may He be blessed. So, he must truly make efforts to strengthen his soul against the power of his materiality, to improve his condition [and] to raise himself up to the measure that is fitting for him.

What man's world and occupation do to him: And the place that he is in is also, material and dark; and all that are found in it are material. So, it is impossible that man's occupation in it and in all that is in it be anything but material and physical. Since they are all material and physical, and the condition of man himself and the composition of his parts force this occupation upon him - for it is impossible for him without eating and drinking and all of the other natural matters, and it is impossible for him without wealth and property so, that he be able to acquire these possessions - it comes out that whether from the angle of man's body or whether from the angle of his world or whether from the angle of man's occupation, he is grounded in materiality and plunged into its darkness. [Hence] he will require great toil and strong effort to rise to a purer condition than this, while he is forced by his nature to [require] these material things.

The material actions become perfect actions: However, it was from the depths of the counsel of His wisdom, may He be blessed, to order the things in such a way that even with man being forcibly plunged into materiality, as we have written, he is able to - from within the materiality itself and from the physical occupation - reach perfection and elevation to purity and distinction. And on the contrary, his being demeaned becomes his being raised. And from there, he will acquire incomparable preciousness and honor - in his changing darkness to light, and gloom to shining brightness. And this is because He, may His name be blessed, placed limits and parameters for man in the use that he can make of the world and its creatures, and in the intention that he intends from them - such that when man uses them within those limits and within those parameters and with that intention that the Creator, may He be blessed, commanded, that physical and material act itself becomes an act of perfection. So, through it, a reality of perfection is realized in man. And he is raised with a great distinction from his lowly condition and becomes elevated from it. [Moreover,] the Supreme Wisdom considered all of the deficiencies implanted in man's makeup and all of the matters of true distinction and preciousness required for him to be fit to cleave to Him, may He be blessed, and enjoy His goodness. And corresponding to all of this, He set up parameters for him and gave him limits; such that if he keeps to them, he will realize all that he needs of the true distinction that we mentioned, and will remove anything that distances him from cleaving to the Most High on account of his makeup. And were it not for the decree that he die, as we have written above, the soul would strengthen itself through these deeds; and the darkness of the body would weaken in such a way as to become completely purified by [the soul]; and they would both rise to cleave to Him, may He be blessed. But since the decree was decreed, the thing is not done at one time. Nevertheless, the soul is strengthened by itself, and the body is purified in [its] potential - even though it is not affected in actuality. So, man acquires the condition of perfection in potential, which comes out later into actuality at the time that is appropriate for it.

And these parameters and limits are the sum of the commandments - the positive and negative commandments - each one of which is intended to acquire and internalize one of the levels of true distinction for man that we mentioned, or to remove one of the matters of darkness or deficiencies, by way of doing that positive commandment or by refraining from the negative commandment. However, the details of all of the commandments - and likewise, the details of each and every commandment - are based upon [man's] true existence and makeup in all of his characteristics and the true matters of perfection that are required, every matter according to its conditions and its limits that are required for its perfection. Truly the Supreme Wisdom - that knows all of this completely and knows all the matters of the creatures and their uses as It truly created them - observed everything and gathered everything that was required for the commandments that It commanded in His Torah. And [this is] as it is written (Deuteronomy 6:24), "And He commanded us to do all of these statutes, etc. for our good, etc."

The root of service (to God): Behold, the root of all matters of service is that man should always turn to his Creator. And that is that he know and understand that he was only created to cleave to his Creator, and that he was only placed in this world to suppress his [evil] inclination and subordinate himself to his Creator with the power of the intellect - the opposite of the desire of materiality and its inclination. So, he should conduct all of his actions to reach this purpose and not incline away from it.

The parts of the service: Truly this conduct is divided into two parts. The first is in that which he does because he was commanded, whereas the second is in that which he does because it is essential and he requires [it]. The explanation of the first is the sum of doing the commandments; and of the second is the sum of what man uses in the world for his needs. The purpose to man of his doing the acts of the commandments is clear - it is to fulfill the commandments of his Creator and to do His will. And behold he fulfills His will, may He be blessed, in two ways that come out from one another. That is that he fulfills His will in that which He commanded him to do this act and he [now] does it. And the second is that through this act, he surely perfects himself in one of the levels of perfection which is the effect of that commandment, as we have written. So, he surely [also] fulfills His will, may He be blessed, in that He desires that man become perfected and arrive at enjoying His good, may He be blessed. And regarding that which man uses from the world for his needs, it must first be limited by the limits of His will, may He be blessed - meaning that there should not be anything in it that God, may He be blessed, prevented [from us] and forbade. And it should only be what is fitting for the health of the body and the preservation of its life in the best possible way; and not according to the inclination towards the material and its desire for extra luxuries. And the intention of this is that the body be ready and prepared, for the soul to use if for the needs of serving his Creator, so, that it not encounters delay from lack of preparation or [from the body's] weakness. And when man uses the world in this way, that use itself becomes an act of perfection, as we have written. And he acquires true distinction from it, as when he acquires [it] by the act of any of the commandments. For this too is a commandment upon us - to preserve our body through proper preparation so, that we can serve our Creator with it and use [things] from this world with that intention and for that purpose, according to that which is required for us. And it comes out that we are elevated through this act, and the world itself is elevated with it - by its being helpful to man in his submission to his Maker.

And see that one of the things that one must increase in himself is the love and fear of his Creator, may He be blessed. And that is that he reflects on the greatness of His loftiness, may He be blessed and the tremendous lowliness of man; and [that] he humbles himself in front of Him, may He be blessed, and be meekened by His loftiness. And he should want and desire to be from those that serve in front of Him, and [by such an association] be praised by His praise and lauded by His greatness. For these are solid ways that draw a man close to his Creator, purify the darkness of the material, make shine the light of the soul and elevate man form one elevation to [another], until he reaches closeness to Him, may He be blessed.

Study of the Torah: Truly, there is one mechanism that God, may He be blessed, gave to us, the level of which is higher than the other mechanisms that bring man close to Him, and that is Torah study. And this is [achieved] with two approaches. The first is the approach of speech and [simple] study; and the second is the approach of [analytical] understanding. For see that in His kindness, may He be blessed, He willed [to] compose for us a composition of words, like that which was decreed by His wisdom, and gave them to us. And this is the totality of the Book of the Torah; and afterwards, the Books of the Prophets. For through the mystical power of these words, the one who pronounces them with holiness and purity with the correct intention - which is the fulfillment of His will, may He be blessed - will achieve high distinction and truly great perfection. And likewise, one who exerts himself to understand and know their explanations which were passed down to us. He will acquire perfection over his perfection according to his effort - all the more so, if he toils to understand their secrets and mysteries. For any matter that he understands will establish and achieve one of the highest levels of distinction and true perfection in his soul. And in all of these [things], it is not only that he just acquires distinction and perfection for himself, but rather all of what exists in creation is distinguished and perfected - generally and individually. [This is] especially [true] with Torah [study].

The effects of commandments and sins: However, the cause of all of the conditions of man - his darkness and his brightness - is the shining of His face, may He be blessed, upon him or His hiding Himself from him, as we wrote above (Part I, On the Purpose of Creation 2). For behold that the more that the Master, blessed be He, shines His countenance, the more purity and perfection descend to one to whom His shining is coming. And according to the measure of shining, so, is the measure of perfection and purity that is drawn after it; and the opposite of this with [His] hiding. However, the Master, may be blessed, always shines upon the one that draws close to Him and there is no withholding of it from His side at all. Rather, the one that does not draw close to him will lack His shining; such that the withholding is from the side of the receiver, and not from the side of the Giver. And behold the Supreme Wisdom decreed that the one who does these things that He commanded - meaning the sum of all of the commandments, as we mentioned above - will come a level closer to Him, may He be blessed, with every such act that he does. And through this, he will reach a higher level of the shining of His countenance, and will achieve a higher level of perfection, which is the effect of that [higher] level of shining. And the opposite [of this occurs with] sins: Every one of those acts that man does, God forbid, surely distances him a certain level from Him, may He be blessed, on account of it. And through this, an additional level of deficiency, which is an effect of this hiding, [comes to him].

It comes out according to all that we have prefaced that the true intention in all of the commandments would be to come close to Him, may He be blessed, and to be enlightened by the light of His countenance. And [the intention] of preventing sins is to escape from being distanced from Him. And this is the true purpose for them. Yet the specific matters are very deep, according to the makeup of man and of the creation, as we wrote above. And we will speak more about some of them in a separate part (Part 4), with the help of God, may He be blessed.

On the Spiritual Realm

The parts of creation: The entire creation is [made up] of two parts - the physical and the spiritual. The physical is that which is perceived by our senses; and it is divided into the higher ones and the lower ones. The higher ones are all of the heavenly objects that determine [events], which are all of the spheres and the stars. The lower ones are all of what is located in the lower sphere - meaning the earth, the water and the air, and all the perceivable bodies that are in them. The spiritual is that which is created devoid of matter [and] cannot be perceived by our senses. [They are also, divided into] two types: One is the souls and the other is the ethereal beings. The soul is a type of spiritual creature that is destined to go into a body and to be integrated with it, and to perform certain acts within it at certain times. The ethereal beings are a specie of spiritual creatures that are not destined for bodies at all. And they are divided [further] into two categories. The first is called powers and the second is called angels. And they too are of many different levels. So, they have different natural axioms about their existence according to their level and their standing, to the point that we can call them many species of one category - that is the angelic category. However, there is one type of creature that is like something between the spiritual and the physical. And that is that it can really not be perceived by our senses, nor is it limited by any physical limits that are perceived, nor [by] its axioms. And from this angle, they are imprecisely called spiritual. But it is distinct from the angelic specie, even though it resembles it in certain respects. And it has its own axioms and specific limits, according to its true reality. And it is called the demonic specie, which is the specie of the demons. And it truly also, has many subdivisions, such that the general specie becomes a category and they are its species. And behold the human specie is distinguished and distinct by itself, in that it is made up of two types of creations that are completely distinct - meaning, the lofty soul and the lowly body - something not found in any other creature. And here you should be careful not to err to think that the makeup of other animals is like the makeup of man. As the spirits in animals are only the most ethereal element of the physical. And its like is also, found in man, since he is an animal. However, besides it all, he [also] has a lofty soul, which is a unique type of creation completely distinct from the body. And it is extremely different than it and very far from it, but it is brought together with it by His decree, may He be blessed, with the intention that we mentioned in the previous chapters.

The head creatures are the powers from which everything is an effect: The physical creatures are known to us, and their axioms and their general natural properties are well-known. However, it is impossible for us to have a proper picture of the spiritual [beings]; as they are beyond our imagination. So, we will only speak about them and their makeup according to the tradition in our hands. And see that among the great principles in our hands about this matter is that there are ethereal powers above, corresponding to everything that is found among the lower beings. It is from them that things unfold and proceed in a single line of cause and effect decreed by His wisdom, may He be blessed. The lower beings - they, their occurrences and their existence - are rooted in these powers; so, these lower beings are extensions and effects of these powers. And one is connected to the other, like rings of a chain [of causation]. Another tradition in our hands is that for every essence and every event among these lower being, supervisors from the angelic category we mentioned above are appointed. And their task is to preserve that essence or that event among the lower things, according to what it is, and to renew that which is appropriate to renew among the lowly beings, according to the Supreme decree.

In truth, the main existence of the world and its true state [occurs] through these higher powers. And the effects of that which [occurs with] them is [what occurs] to the lower physical beings. And this is whether it is beginning its creation, or it is developing as time passes. And this means that according to what is created from these powers, the order in which they are set and the limits that have been set up, that is what unfolds afterwards according to the axiom of unfolding that the Creator, may His name be blessed, willed. And according to that which develops and will develop among them, is what develops and will develop among the lower creatures. Whereas the existence, condition, arrangement and all of the other distinctions among [the higher] powers are according to that which is appropriate for them in accordance with their true makeup; the existence, condition, arrangement and all of the other occurrences among the lower beings, unfold [from the spiritual beings] and are applied to that which is appropriate in them according to their true natures.

Three general processes in creation: See that according to this root concept, the beginning of all events is above with the higher powers and their end is below with the lower creatures. And likewise, the beginning of all developments is above and their end is below. However, there is one component that is an exception to this rule. And that is that which relates to man's free choice. For since the Master, may His name be blessed, wanted that man have the power to choose what he wants of good or evil, He made him independent of others. And just the opposite, [God] gave him the power to actually move the world and its creatures, according to that which he chooses with his will. So, it comes out that there are two opposite general processes in the world: The first is natural and determined, whereas the second is chosen; the first is top-down, and the second is bottom-up. The one that is determined is the process by which the lower being are moved by the higher powers and this is certainly top-down. The one that is chosen is that which man moves through his free will. But it is surely impossible that that which he moves be anything but something physical - for man is physical and his actions are physical. However, because of the connection and interaction that exists between the higher powers and physical things - movement of the physical brings about an eventual effect upon the higher power that is above it. So, it comes out that that this process is bottom-up, the opposite of the determined one that we mentioned. However, you should know that not even man himself chooses all of his actions. Rather some of them are from his choice, while others are caused by a Supreme decree for his reward or his punishment (and as we will write in its place, with God's help [in Part 2, On Personal Providence 4]). Yet the property of that which follows from a decree that is upon him is like other matters of the world, the process of which is top-down - like that which is moved by the higher powers. But that which is coming from the angle of his free choice will move bottom-up, as we have explained.

But note that the Master, blessed be He, has arranged that all matters upon which man has free choice will move the [higher] powers according to the measure and the level that He established. This is the case, since it is not only [man's] actions that move [things], but also, his speech and even his thoughts; yet the measure and level of the movement will only be according to that limit that the Supreme Wisdom decreed and set up.

However, after the process moved by choice [begins], it will perforce bring a determinate process. For once it has moved the higher powers, by [the actions] of man, they go back and move the lower beings with the unfolding of the natural process [that they put into] motion. Nevertheless, there are many specific properties to all of these things according to what the Supreme Wisdom, in the depth of His counsel, decreed would be appropriate for His creation - to measure out all the many measures, both in the contact of the process from man to the powers, and in the contact of the process of the powers to the lower beings. According to these deep secrets do all the mechanisms of His direction, may He be blessed, cause everything that was and will be.

The beginning of good and evil in the root powers: And note that since His Wisdom, may He be blessed, decreed that good and bad exist in the world - as we explained - the beginning of this thing must surely be in these root forces. And after them, the thing continues to the lower beings. And see that His Wisdom, may He be blessed, arranged that the ethereal powers [include] the roots of the creations, that we mentioned, in proper order and fashion; such that they experience wholeness and corruption according to that which is appropriate for them - meaning that there be a state of good and not good in them. And the actualization of the good state is that [the power] be prepared to be illuminated by the light of His countenance, may He be blessed, and that He shine upon them. And the opposite is that this preparation be lacking from them, and that He be hidden from them. And the effect of their wholeness in the lower beings is the good. And the opposite is the opposite.

Created powers as the cause for the doing of evil: And you need to know that even though it is surely true that the cause of all good things in every place - meaning whether in the higher powers or in their outgrowths - is surely the emanation of His countenance, may He be blessed, and the cause of evil in every place is the hiding of His emanation; nevertheless [only] for the good is the Master, blessed be He, described as the actual cause to its principles and its components. But as for the evil, we do not describe Him, may His name be blessed, as the actual cause. For the Holy One, blessed be He, truly does not combine His name with evil. Rather it is the hiding of His light and the covering of His countenance that is considered its root. For that is its true cause; hence [evil] is actually the removal of good. However, the Master, blessed be He - who is omnipotent and who has no impediment to His will and no limit whatsoever to His ability - made a root and a specific source for the components of the contents of its existence, dedicated to this purpose of the expression of the components of evil, according to that which the Supreme Wisdom determined to be necessary for the desirable state for man and the world. And this is what is stated by the verse (Isaiah 45:7), "I form light and create darkness, I make weal and create evil." And the makeup of this root is the sum of the various powers. All of the matters of lacking and evil unfold from them in all of their aspects, whether regarding things that relate to the soul or that relate to the body in all of their components and sections. And we will still speak [more] about this in Part II (On Specific Modes of Providence 2), with God's help. And see that the sum of these powers is activated to act or not to act - whether in all of it or in sections of it - according to the hiding of His light, may He be blessed, and the covering of His countenance. For according to the measure of the hiding is the measure that the sum of these powers, or sections of them, will be given control and power to act. And surely when these powers gain strength and are empowered, the strength of the good will be weakened and the state of the root powers of the creatures that we mentioned will be corrupted; and they and their extensions will be weakened. But when these powers are subdued and control and action is taken away from them, the good is strengthened and the roots of the creatures are made whole. And they become stabilized in the state of the good, so, they and their extensions will be strengthened. However, the root of all of the matters that we mentioned - from the matters of good and evil, the war of the intellect and the material, and all the matters of wholeness and corruption - is the bolstering of these powers and the reaching of their input and effects upon the creatures, in [their] roots and [their] extensions; or their being subdued, and the negation of their action and the removal of their input and effect from the creatures, [their] roots and [their] extensions.

And there are surely many different levels about the matter of the powers of evil that we mentioned, and that which is influenced by them. And generally, that which is influenced by them is called impurity, darkness, pollution, mundane or that which is similar. And that which is influenced by the shining of His countenance, may He be blessed, is called holiness, purity, light, blessing and that which is similar to it. But when we distinguish the component matters, we will distinguish all of these types and their components, according to which the Master's oversight, blessed be He, with which He directs His world, depends.

Angels put everything into effect: Nevertheless, for every one of these matters, there are surely supervisors of the angelic specie appointed, as we explained above, to put the thing into effect into physicality - whether for the good, or not for the good. And behold these are His servants, may He be blessed, who preform His word. As so, did He will and arrange that His decrees go out into action through His angels, according to what He ordered and gave over to them.

Part Two

On Divine Providence in General

It is well-known and clear that all of the creatures that were created - both the higher ones and the lower ones - were surely created because the Supreme Wisdom saw a need and a function for them for the general purpose of the world. And all of their natural axioms and properties were set and embedded, according to what the Supreme Wisdom decreed to be appropriate, according to the intention that It intended for that creature. However, for that very reason itself that they were created, it is also, fit that they by preserved the whole time that they have that function for the general creation, as I have written. And therefore, the Master, blessed be He, that created all of these creatures will also, not stop from supervising over them, to preserve them in the state that He wants them to be.

His providence, may He be blessed, over all levels of creation: However, we have already prefaced in Part I, Chapter 5 (On the Spiritual Realm 3) that the beginning of all the creatures are the ethereal beings; and from them do the physical things unfold. And all the physical things in all of their components are according to that which is forwarded to them from those powers in their various aspects. And there is nothing big or small among the physical things that does not have a cause and root in the ethereal beings, according to their [various] aspects. And the Master, may He be blessed, is certainly overseeing over all of these matters according to [how] He created them - meaning, first upon the ethereal beings and upon all of their processes according to what they actually are. And likewise, does He also, oversee the appointees that He appointed, over those which [physically] exist - as we mentioned there - to preserve them and their missions and to continually give them the power to accomplish their deeds.

His providence over the human specie: However, since the human specie is differentiated from all the other species, in that he is given free choice and the ability to acquire that which is perfection or deficiency for himself - and in this regard, acts and impacts, and is not impacted upon - the oversight over him must also, be differentiated from the oversight over the other species: Behold, it is necessary to oversee and observe the components of his actions and to furnish him [with conditions that] correspond to his ways and are like the fruit of his deeds. So, it comes out that all of his actions and their outgrowths are overseen; and that, in return, he is supervised according to that which is appropriate for the outgrowths of these actions with specificity - measure for measure - and as we shall write further. And that is something not relevant with the other species that are acted upon and do not act (independently), so, they are not fit for perfection except for that which is for that specie [as a whole], according to that source that it has as it source. For there is surely oversight to preserve that root and its extensions, according to that which its nature, its axiom and its root determine it should be. But the human specie, the individuals of which act and impact, as we have written, must certainly be overseen individually according to what their actions cause them - no more and no less. And we will still expand the explanation of this thing further, with God's help.

On Mankind in This World

Regarding matters of this world as a preparation for the world to come: Behold we have already prefaced that given that the purpose of the creation of the human species is that he should merit and reach the true good - which is cleaving to Him, may He be blessed, in the world to come - it comes out that the end of all of his processes is surely the repose of the world to come. Nevertheless, the Supreme Wisdom decreed that it is fit and seemly that before this, his state in this world would be tied and limited by the natural axioms of this world, such that it be a true and proper preparation to reach the desired purpose. And according to this root principle, He arranged all the matters of this world to be preparation and training for that which will be afterwards in the final world, which is the world to come.

The end of the processes of the human specie: Yet this preparation hinges upon two poles; the first being personal and the second, communal. The personal is the matter of the acquisition of his perfection through his actions. And the communal is that the human specie as a whole prepares itself for life in the world to come. And the explanation of this matter is that the human specie is created with a good impulse and an evil impulse, so, it is not impossible for parts of it to be good and parts of it to be bad. However, the end of the process must be that the evil ones will be pushed off, and that the good ones be gathered and made into one group. For the true good that is attained in the world to come is destined for this group.

The division of repayment into two time periods and two places: However, the axiom of free choice that automatically results in the possibility that we mentioned among the parts of the human specie - that they be good or bad, or likewise, that some of them be good and some of them be bad - itself also, automatically results in this possibility among the actions of each individual within the human specie. Hence it is possible that all of them be good or all of them be bad, but it is [also] possible that some of them be good and some of them be bad. And this is from what impedes the group of [the good] ones that we mentioned. For there are truly good matters and bad matters found in one individual himself. And to pay attention to only some of [their actions] and not to the others - even if the ones that are given attention are the majority - is surely not from righteous judgement. For exact [justice] would require that all actions be repaid - whether they be large or small, many or few. Hence the Supreme Wisdom decreed to divide the repayment - for both reward and punishment - into two times and two places. This means that the sum of [a person's] actions be divided between the majority and the minority; and that the majority be judged by itself in the place and time that is appropriate for it, and the minority be judged by itself in the place and time that is appropriate for it. However,, the true and main repayment will be in the world to come, as I have written: That the reward will be for the man who has merited to live on eternally, to cleave to Him, may He be blessed, forever; and the punishment is to be pushed away from the true good and to perish. However, the judgement for this matter will only be according to the majority of the actions. However, the [repayment] for the good deeds of the evildoer and the bad deeds of the righteous - being that they are the minority - will be found in this world, through his successes and his woes. For though it will the evildoer receive repayment for the little merit that he has, through his successes; and the righteous one will receive the punishment of his iniquities, through [his] afflictions in it - such that, in this manner, judgement be perfect for all. So, the makeup of the world to come will remain as it should be in that perfect state. That means that the righteous ones will remain by themselves, without an admixture of evildoers among them. And they will be without impediments, from themselves, for the enjoyment destined for them; whereas the evildoers will be pushed away and perish, without there remaining any claim for them at all.

Geihinnom (Purgatory) and other spiritual punishments: However, His Kindness, may He be blessed, also, decreed, to increase salvation for people, that there be another type of purging for whoever the purging is possible - meaning for one in whom evil was very strong, but not so, much so, that his verdict be to have him completely perish. And that is a group of punishments, the most noted of which is judgement in Geihinnom (Purgatory). And the intent of it is to punish the sinner according to his sins in such a way that - after his punishment - he has no more liability for the evil act that he did, so, that he be able to receive the true reward afterwards, according to his remaining good deeds. And according to this, it comes out that those that perish will be scant [and] not abundant. For behold they will only be those in which the measure of evil became so, great as to be impossible in any way that a place be found for them to remain [for] true repayment and eternal enjoyment. And see that it comes out that judgement is divided into three parts. As its main [part] is in the world after resurrection, as we have written. However, actions are fit to be repaid before then. Behold there are those of them that will be repaid in this world and those that will be repaid in the world of souls. In truth, the elements of the properties of this judgment are only known to the true Judge alone. For He is the one who knows the true essence of actions and their outgrowths and details; and He knows which one of them is fitting to repay at a [certain] time and in a [certain] way, and which at a different time and in a different way. And that which we do know is only the general ways of [God's] direction - upon what it is based and what it is causing. And [the latter] is that which we explained, that the purpose of the whole matter is to gather an eternal group for cleaving to Him, may He be blessed. And in order for this matter to be perfected as is fit, all of these earlier matters were necessary to prepare and make ready this ultimate goal, as we have written.

The mystical power of afflictions: And behold that when you delve still deeper into this matter, you will see that besides this matter being a consequence based on judgement and righteousness - as we have written - it is also, based upon the reality of creation. For we have already explained that good deeds actualize within man - in his body and in his soul - a reality of perfection and distinction. And their opposite with evil deeds - they actualize a reality of murkiness and deficiency. And everything is exactly according to what the deeds are - no less and no more. And behold the righteous man who invested himself with a great measure of splendor and distinction, but - from another angle, because of the few bad deeds that he did - has a small admixture of darkness and murkiness: So, long as he has this admixture in him, he is not ready and fit to cleave to Him, may He be blessed. Hence the Supreme Kindness decreed that there be a purging for him. And that is the sum of the afflictions that He, may He be blessed, [ordered] - with their mystical powers - to rid this man of that murkiness and remain pure and shiny, ready for the good at the fitting time. However, according to the measure of murkiness that the man acquired from his actions, so, will be the afflictions that are required for his purging. And it is [also] possible that there is not enough power in the afflictions to remove the murkiness from him and he will require spiritual afflictions. And the general rule is divided into many components - it is impossible for man's intellect to encompass them all.

The merit of evildoers is completely in this world: But complete evildoers are the ones within whom the evil of their deeds brings about so, great a murkiness and darkness that their bodies and souls are truly corrupted. And they are then not fit in any way to cleave to Him, may He be blessed. But note that it is possible that a few good deeds be found in their hands; but these are deeds, such that when they go up on His righteous scales, may He be blessed, do not tip [them] to the side of the true good at all - not from the angle of their quantity and not from the angle of their quality. As behold if they would tip them towards it, they would no longer be considered complete evildoers, but rather from those who undergo purging until they reach a state that is prepared for the good. Nevertheless so, that [God's] attribute of [strict] justice not be lacking - such that these deeds not be rewarded - it was designed that their reward be given to them in this world, as we have written. So, it comes out that this merit is finished and it does not suffice to actualize any true distinction in them.

There are levels in the group of those destined for the world to come: However, there is one more very central component to this matter, and that is that in the group of the perfect ones that we mentioned will be in the world to come, the intent is not that they will all be on one level and one status and reach the same success. Rather the thing is that the Supreme Wisdom measured where the last end would reach - meaning the lowest measure of cleaving to Him, may He be blessed, and the [resultant] enjoyment within one's [own] perfection. And corresponding to this, He set up that anyone whose actions reach this small measure may already be counted among the group that we mentioned and be among those remaining to derive enjoyment from [Him]. Nevertheless, one who did not even reach this is surely pushed off completely, and perishes. However, whoever merits more will surely be greater and higher in that group. And it was from the depth of His counsel, may He be blessed, that man completely be his own benefactor - whether in general or specifically. The explanation of this is that it is not sufficient that he not merits the good until after his toil, but rather that even the specific portion that is given to him be only exactly according to his deeds. And it comes out that a person will only be on the level that he chose and within which he placed himself there on his own. And there are indeed higher ones and lower ones, great ones and little ones in this gathering. Yet there will not be another reason for the high level of a man or its lowness, its greatness or its smallness, besides he himself; such that he not have a grievance with another at all.

The law of man's level in the group of those destined for the world to come: Yet according to this root, you find another great distinction in the judgement of deeds - to judge [which deeds] are fit to have effects upon the advancement of a person in the group of the perfect ones that we mentioned; and the measure of the advancement that they will be given. For there are in fact deeds found that do not suffice to give a person advancement in that world, according to the exacting and righteous supreme justice. Rather they will be rewarded in this world - so, that such a man will be among the lower eternal ones, among the small ones of that group. And behold this is a little similar to those that we mentioned above that receive their reward in this world and perish for the world to come. However, they are distinguished from them by a great difference. And that is that those we mentioned - who are the complete evildoers - have all the power of their good deeds completely cease with the reward in this world, and do not reach eternity at all; whereas the deeds of [the former] surely bring them to eternity. And even if they will need very much purging, they nevertheless have a share in the eternal remnant. However, because of the corruption of their deeds, their [fulfillment of the] commandments only brings them to receive that small portion that we mentioned, whereas many of their merits receive their [reward] in this world. For had it been in line with justice for them to be repaid for [those deeds] in the world to come and not in this world, these people would have truly found themselves in one of the higher levels of the group of the perfected ones.

However, everything that we have mentioned up until now is explaining the matter of the afflictions of the righteous in this world and the tranquility of the evildoers - as well as the spiritual punishments - from the angle of preparation for the true reward of the world to come. Yet the reward of the righteous in this world follows a different path, and it remains ahead [of us] with God's help. So, all that we have explained is according to the second general pole that we mentioned, for preparation. But the matters that follow the personal pole, work with a different procedure than all of this. And we will explain it now in a chapter of its own, with God's help.

On Personal Providence

The assignments given to people in this world: Behold we have already prefaced that the [divine] service given over to man is dependent on matters of good and evil having been created in the world and man being placed between them, for him to choose the good. Yet the matters of good are many, as are the matters of evil. For is not every good trait within the good, and the opposite for every bad trait? By way of example, pride is from the matters of evil and humility is from the matters of good; mercy is from the matters of good and cruelty is its opposite; contentment and happiness in one's portion are from the good matters and its opposite is from the evil matters. And likewise, with all the other individual traits. And see that the Supreme Wisdom determined all of the specifics of this type that would be fitting to exist, and to allow for their possibility in human nature - according to the main purpose that we mentioned in its place. And [God] created them, all their aspects, their causes, their effects and all that accompanies them; and He implanted their possibility in man, as we have written. However, for all of these matters to exist, it was necessary to have different states among people - such that they all be a test for them, in that there be room for all of these specific aspects of evil, and that there be room for man to strengthen himself against them and to seize the good. By way of example, if there were no rich people and poor people, there would be no chance for a person to have mercy and not be cruel. But now the rich person is tested with his wealth, whether he will be cruel to the poor person that needs him or have mercy upon him. And likewise, the poor person will be tested, whether he will be contented with the little in his hand and be thankful to his God or the opposite. The wealth [itself] will also, be a test to the rich person, whether his heart will become proud from it and whether he will be drawn through it to the vanities of the world and leave the service of his Creator; or if, with all of his wealth, he will [still] be humble and subdued and disgusted by the vanities of this world and nevertheless choose [to be involved with] the Torah and [with divine] service. And likewise, anything that is similar to this. However, the Supreme Wisdom divided all these types of tests among individuals of the human specie, as His deep counsel found to be be fitting and proper. And it comes out that each and every individual of the human specie has their specific portion of testing and fight with the [evil] impulse, and that is his assignment and load in this world; and he must endure it according to that which it is. And his actions will [then] be judged by His trait of justice, may He be blessed, according to the load that he was truly given in all of its aspects with utmost exactitude. And behold this is like the servants of the king that all stand ready for his discipline; and among all of them, they must fulfill the work of his kingdom. And so, he divides a certain portion to each one of them, such that all of the parts that are needed by him will be finished. And behold that each one takes upon himself to complete that portion that is given over to him, and the king will repay him according the performance of his assignment. Yet [when it comes to God,] the measure of this division and its ways are much too lofty for our grasp and it is impossible for us to fathom them. Rather only the Supreme Wisdom, that is loftier than any intellect, is what measured it and arranged it in the most perfect way.

See that the matters of the world all flow and move, by unfolding from one matter to the next; from their existence in the ethereal beings to their existence in the physical word, as I wrote in Part I, Chapter 5 (The Spiritual Realm 3). [Accordingly,] all of these things - the details of man's testing, as I mentioned - begin in the root of its aspect in the ethereal beings, according to the reality of improvement and corruption that is relevant to them, as I have written above. And they are meted out and determined to exist and to spread into physicality in the individuals that are fit for them; until all the details of existence are arranged according to this property of division [of the various tests] in their various

Derech   Part Two   **Hashem**

levels. And the Supreme Wisdom looks over all of them and decrees what is most fitting according to their true existence. And this is clear according to the general principles with which we prefaced [this discussion].

The assignments given to man in this world: It comes out according to this root principle that the successes of this world and its troubles are in order for man to be tested by them with the types of tests that the Supreme Wisdom determined to be appropriate for this individual.

Events in this world to help or hinder the acquisition of perfection: However, there is another factor that comes into play according to the ways of judgement and reward. And that is that the Supreme Judge decreed that - as a result of man's own actions - He, may He be blessed, will assist to make the achievement of his perfection easier for him and to save him from obstacles, as the matter is stated (I Samuel 2:9), "He guards the footsteps of His faithful." Of course, there are many levels in this: As one will find that the principle of justice will allow, that according to the actions that one person has already done, the Creator, may He be Praised, will help him a little; and someone else who He will help more, such that He will greatly help him achieve perfection; and still someone else that He will help even more. And likewise, the opposite: One who already according to [the ways of] justice is fit not to be helped from the Heavens, However, perfection is not made more difficult for him; and another whose judgement goes out, such that obstacles are increased for him, so, he will require strength and toil in order to achieve it; and there is yet another - who is a complete evildoer - from whom all the ways of improvement are sealed and will be pushed off in his evil. And there are many, many fine details in all of these things. And so, note that it is possible that a man merits that successes in this world are decreed upon him to help him in his service, so, that it be easier for him to accomplish the perfection he seeks, and that no obstacles get in his way. And it is [also] possible that losses and troubles be decreed upon him according to his deeds, to stand like a wall in front of him and intervene between him and perfection - to the point that he will need more toil and discomfort to bore through that burrow and make efforts, regardless of all of his preoccupations, to nevertheless accomplish his perfection. And the opposite with an evildoer: It is possible that successes will be decreed about him to open the gate of perdition in front of him, that he be pushed off through it. But it [also] possible that troubles be decreed about him to prevent him from the evil that he intended to do. And that will happen when the Supreme Director will know that it is not appropriate for that evildoer to do it for whatever reason. And [about] this did David pray (Psalms 140:9), "Do not, O Lord, grant the desires of the wicked; do not let their plan succeed." And behold He, may His name be blessed, does all of these matters in His amazing wisdom; everything according to what is appropriate for the collective of His creatures, as I have written. And He judges creatures in all of their circumstances according to what they truly are - meaning to say, one who is in a state of comfort and is negligent in his service is not the same as one who is in a state of duress and preoccupied by the pressures upon him and, so, does not achieve perfection. Hence their judgement will surely not be the same. Rather each one will be judged according to what he truly is - whether inadvertent or volitional; whether he is forced or does it willingly. And He, may His name be blessed, knows the truth of all words, deeds and thoughts, and judges them accordingly.

Afflictions - for arousal: However, there is another extension of this principle regarding afflictions: For it also, possible that a man be righteous but have sins in his hand - or be average with his actions evenly divided - such that the decree upon him is to arouse him to repent. And see that he will be afflicted from the Heavens so, that he pays attention and examine his deeds. However, these afflictions are not from the afflictions of atonement that we mentioned above, the point of which is to remove the iniquities in this world. Rather these afflictions are afflictions of arousal, to arouse the heart to repentance. For punishments were actually only designed for when there is no repentance. But what He, may He be blessed, desires is that man not sin; and that if he sin, he repent. But if he does not repent - in order that he not be destroyed - he is purged by punishments. And so, the premise of afflictions is the potential for arousal. But if man is not aroused by them, he is then afflicted with afflictions that remove [the sins]. And about this matter, Elihu said (Job 36:10), "He opens their understanding by discipline, and orders them back from mischief."

The filling of the measure: And you should know that there is a limit given to the evildoer, until what point he be allowed to continue doing evil, according to his choice of evil. But when he reaches that limit, there will not be any delay at all, and he will be destroyed from upon the face of the earth. And that is what the Sages, may their memory be blessed, called "filling the measure"; and what Scripture [refers to when it] states (Job 20:22), "When he has all he wants, trouble will come." But before that time, it is surely possible that he continues to succeed for the reason that we mentioned above - that is to open the gate of perdition for him. And that is what they, may their memory be blessed, wrote (Yoma 38b), "[For] one who comes to impurify, they open [the gate] for him." However, when he reaches that limit, he has already reached perdition and will be destroyed. Then the fiery anger of the Lord will be upon him; and devastation, through which he will be destroyed, will come upon him.

Events [that happen] to a man because of his relations: You should also, know that the Supreme Providence pays attention in every fine detail to all that is connected to him, to those that preceded him and those that will follow him. And in the end, Providence oversees all the details with relationship to the entire collective, from the perspective of all that the parts combine with each part of the collective structure. And among that which is overseen in the judgement of an individual is his standing and state with regards to that which preceded him, meaning the ancestors;

and what will follow him, meaning the children; and that which is with him, meaning the members of the generation, or the citizens of the town or members of his society. And after all of these considerations, he is allotted a portion in the service and in being tested - as mentioned above - and is given his load to serve before Him, may He be blessed. (However, you should surely note that this is only regarding the judgement of this world, being that which I said that his portion in service is decreed. [This] means in which state he will be found in this world, such that his load will be according to that state. However, in the world to come, a man will only be judged according to his [own] deeds, according to the state he was in. And that is what the prophet wrote [Ezekiel 18:20], "a child will not die for the iniquity of the father.") And behold this is because if a man merits that he be granted fame and fortune, his children that will be born to him will be born wealthy. And if nothing new transpires (all other things being equal), they will be rich and famous [as well]; and likewise, the opposite. It comes out that wealth only came to those children from the angle of their being the children of those parents. And it is truly the case that a man bequeaths five things to his children, as they, may their memory be blessed, enumerated (Mishnah Eduyot 2:9). And it it already possible that a man be created with bounty as a result of his father already being endowed with it; and it is also, possible that as a result of his father's merit, bounty will come to him at a certain time, or the opposite. On the other hand, it is possible that salvation or bounty be granted to him for the progeny that will come from him in the future. And likewise, is it possible that bounty or evil, from the goods and lackings of this world, be granted to him because of his place or his society.

Afflictions to the righteous for the good of their generation or for the good of all the world: However, besides all of this, there is another matter that follows from the two parts of [divine] direction that we mentioned - the personal and the communal. And that is that the Supreme Wisdom surely looked down upon all that was fit to be present for the improvement of the species from which It would make a group of the perfected ones that we mentioned above, and saw that it would be very good for them, that there be power in some of them to help others and benefit them. [This] means that the matter not be absolute, that only one who comes to perfection from his own ability be from those counted in the group of those in the world to come. Rather even one whose actions have brought him [to a point] that, if he were to be accompanied by someone else more worthy than him, he could benefit from perfection - can enter into this category. However, he will be on the lowest level, which is the level of one dependent upon his fellow. And it comes out that the only one to be completely pushed off from perfection is the one who is not fit to enjoy from it - not on account of himself and not on account of being accompanied by someone else. And through this, salvation is more plentiful, and more [individuals] benefit. However, those that benefit and cause others to benefit are certainly greater in the group, and will be the leaders. And those that need to be accompanied by them will be subservient to them and will require them. And in order that there be a place for this great refinement, [God] connected the individuals, one with the other, from the beginning. And this is the matter of "All of Israel are guarantors for one another," that they, may their memory be blessed, mentioned (Shevuot 39a). For through this, they are surely found to be connected with each other, and not [be in a situation of] each person separated for himself. And surely the good trait is always greater; such that since they are [punished], one for the other, with sin; all the more so, does one effect the other with merit. However, according to this principle, it is set up that troubles and afflictions may come to a righteous man, and it be as atonement for his generation. And behold the righteous are obligated to lovingly accept the afflictions that are prepared for them for the benefit of their generation, as one of them would lovingly accept the afflictions that would be fit for him on his own account. And with this action, he benefits his generation; since he atones for it. And he himself ascends a great deal, as he is made into one of the leaders of the group of those who will be in the world to come, as we have mentioned. However, in this very same category, there is another one of even greater stature than the one we [just] mentioned. And that is because the one we mentioned is when the righteous man be struck for the people of his generation who were fit for a very great punishment and they were close to annihilation or destruction; so, he atones for them with his afflictions and saves them in this world and helps them also, in the world to come. However, there are other afflictions that are given to the greatest of the pious who have already perfected themselves. And they are to help that which is necessary for all of the processes of the direction [of the world] to reach their end - which is perfection. And the explanation of the matter is that surely from the angle of the original arrangement that was designed for the direction of the world and its processes, there was already a need for man to suffer a little pain, in order for him - along with all of the world - to reach perfection. And that is what arises and proceeds as a result of the concealment of His light, may He be blessed, and the hiding of His countenance which He set down as one of the foundations of the conditions of man's state, as we have written earlier. And all the more is this so, once corruptions proliferated in the world - from the perspective of sins upon great and enormous sins that were done in it - such that hiddenness increased and the good was concealed. And it comes out that the world and its creatures are in a lowly and bad state. And it is nevertheless necessary that through the processes that His amazing Wisdom unfurled, matters reach their refinement. And among the fundamental processes is that men should receive punishments according to their evil [deeds] until the [divine] trait of justice is satisfied. However, the Master, blessed be He, arranged that the perfect and important ones could repair [matters] for the sake of others, as we have written; and that the trait of justice would strike them instead of striking the whole world. Nevertheless, since they themselves are perfect and are only being afflicted for the sake of others, it is certain that the trait of justice will be satisfied with a little from them in the place of much from the sinners themselves. Moreover, through this, their merit increases and their power is strengthened. And all the more so, are they able to 'repair that which others have twisted.' So, not only will they repair what is from the people of their generation, but will also, [do so] for all that the world has been corrupted - from when there were [first] sins upon it, up until now. And they will certainly afterwards be the heads of the leaders in the group of the perfected, and the closest ones to Him, may He be blessed.

But behold all that we have mentioned until now according to the angle of justice is also, understood from the angle of what [needs to] occur, according to the truth of its arrangements, as we have written above. For note that with sins, pollution is increased and strengthened among people, and it causes His light, may He be blessed, to be hidden and concealed, with one concealment after another. And according to the removal of this pollution and the purification of the creatures from it; so, does His light, may He be blessed, return and reveal one revelation after another. However, the afflictions are what removes the pollution - whether for individuals or for the group. So, through the afflictions of these important ones, it is continually removed from the whole entire creation, such that the world approaches perfection - one level after another.

Afflictions to a man from the reincarnation of his soul: There is [yet] another principle found in the direction of the matters of this world. And that is that the Supreme Wisdom arranged to expand salvation more, as we have mentioned, such that one soul comes to this world at various times in different bodies. And behold through this, it may repair at a different time what it corrupted in a [previous] time; or perfect what it did not perfect. However, at the end of all the incarnations in the judgement in the future to come, the trial will surely be regarding [the soul], according to all of the incarnations that it experienced and all the states in which it existed. And behold it is possible that matters will occur to a person whose soul was reincarnated according to that which was caused to it from the angle of what it did in a previous incarnation. And the state [of affairs] in the world given to this man is according to this. And according to the condition that he is given will be the load incumbent upon him, as we mentioned earlier. But His judgement, may He be blessed, is exact upon each person according to what he is, in all of his aspects - meaning in all aspects of his [various] states. [This is] such that He will never burden a man in the world to come - which is the true good - with guilt that he does not really have. Rather what comes to him is from the load and assignment in this world which the Supreme Wisdom distributed to him; and his actions are judged according to that. And see that there are many specific details found in this matter of reincarnation - how a man is judged according to what he is in his incarnation and according to what preceded in another incarnation; such that all of it be according to true justice and righteousness. And about this is it stated (Deuteronomy 32:4), "The Rock's act is perfect; all of His ways are justice, etc." And the creations do not have the knowledge that can absorb His thoughts, may His name be blessed, nor the depth of His counsel. We only know this principle like [we know] all of the principles - that one of the causes of people's occurrences in this world is reincarnation - according to the righteous statutes that were legislated in front of Him, may He be blessed - for the perfection of this entire matter.

Events are not the result of several causes: According to all that we have explained, there are various different causes found for the occurrences of people in this world - whether for the good or the bad. However, the matter is not that every occurrence that happens is a result of all of these causes. Rather the matter is that [the sum of the] occurrences that happen to people in the world are from all of these causes; but one occurrence comes from one cause and others come from another cause. So, the Supreme Wisdom that always knows and looks over what is proper for the refinement of the whole creation surely weighs all of the things together in the depth of Its counsel. And It directs the world in all of its details according to this. For it is indeed impossible for all of these causes to all produce their effects at once. For many times, it is possible that one contradicts its fellow. As behold - by way of illustration - even though wealth is coming to a person according to the merit of [his] ancestors; according to his actions, poverty is coming to him; whereas according to the general division, wealth or poverty. And even just according to the actions themselves, the judgement of one action would be that it would bring him a certain good, while the judgement of [another] action would be that he should lack that good. However, the Supreme Wisdom weighs and determines everything according to what is best and furnishes each and every person with things of one type and things of another - meaning things resulting from one of the causes and things resulting from another cause. However, no occurrence happens to a man that is not from one of these causes that we mentioned. Yet it is impossible for a man to know all of the details; and we already know much when we know the principles of the various matters, as we have written.

Events as means and as ends: However, you should know that there are two types of occurrences that happen to people. The first is occurrences that are ends and the second is occurrences that are means. The understanding of ends is occurrences that are decreed upon a person because they are appropriate for him from the angle of one of the causes that we mentioned above. Whereas means are occurrences that happen to him so, that another occurrence that is appropriate for him will come to him. And this is like the matter of "I will thank You, O Lord, for You were angry with me" (Isaiah 12:1), which they, may their memory be blessed, explained [is about one] whose cow broke its leg and fell, and he found a treasure underneath it; or one who escaped from an occurrence which should not have come his way - such as if he delayed and hence did not leave on a boat upon which he wanted to leave, and the boat sunk (Niddah 31a). And even these means are possible that they occur to him for his sake or for the sake of someone else, such that, through this, a good or evil will come to that someone. However, just like the Supreme Wisdom will determine the matters that are appropriate to come to a person, It will also, determine the means by which it will come to him - until everything is decreed with the utmost exactitude about what is truly the best thing.

On Israel and the Nations

From the deepest matters in His direction [of the world], may He be blessed, is that matter of Israel and the [other] nations of the world. For from the angle of man's nature they truly appear to be the same; but from the angle of the Torah, they are completely and greatly different - distinct like two completely differing species. And behold we will now give a sufficient explanation about this matter, and explain in what they are similar to one another and in what they are different from one another.

The fitting state for Adam and his offspring and what happened to them: The first man (Adam) before his sin was in a much more elevated state than man now, and we already explained this matter (Part 1, On Mankind 6). And in that state, mankind was on a very respectable level, a level fit for perpetual elevation, as we mentioned. And if he had not sinned, he would have perfected himself and further raised himself, one elevation after another. And in that good state, he would have surely had a number of offspring determined by His Wisdom, may He be blessed, according to the truth of what is appropriate for the perfection of those benefiting from His goodness, may He be blessed; and they would have all benefited from that good with him. However, these offspring that were appropriate to come from him were decreed and determined by Him to be at various levels. The explanation of this is that there would be central ones and ancillary ones, roots and branches, these following those in a specific order - like trees with their branches, with the number of trees and the number of branches all determined with total precision. But see that with his sin, he descended greatly from his level and internalized a large amount from the darkness and the murkiness, as we mentioned above. And the whole human specie descended from its level and stood on a very lowly level which was not fit for the perpetually lofty status for which it was first destined. So, he only remained ready and prepared for a much lower level. And in this respect, he produced offspring in the world that were all on this lowly level that we mentioned. However, from the angle of his true root, the existence of the higher aspect, that was the aspect that had been in this specie at the time of his corruption, was nevertheless not extinct from the category of the human specie. So, Adam was not completely pushed off, so, that he could not return to the high level. Rather, he was found on the lower level in actuality, but on the higher level in potential. And behold the Master, may He be blessed, placed the choice in front of these generations that were found at that time, to strengthen themselves and make efforts to elevate themselves from the lowly level and to place themselves on the higher level. And He left them time for this thing, according to what the Supreme Wisdom determined to be appropriate for this effort - in the same way It allows us now to be achieving perfection, and a position among the group of people that will be in the world to come, as we he have written above. For note that anything that has any [allotment for] effort much have a limit to it.

The effort allowed people after the sin (of Adam) until the dispersion (of the Tower of Babel) and the content of the dispersion: Behold that the Supreme Wisdom saw that it was appropriate that this effort be divided between the roots and the branches. This means that at first there would be time for the efforts of the roots, and afterwards for their branches. For all of the human species still needed that its character be set as was appropriate, and to be refined from the corruptions that went into it. And according to the order of levels, it was surely appropriate to first set up the roots and heads of the generations of man to stand on a refined level - for them and their branches. For branches always follow after the root. And behold It limited this time for the effort of the roots, for someone (from any of those existing at that time, as this gate was [wide] open and this matter was attainable for them) to merit and establish himself as fit, to be fixed as the one good and precious root that is fit for the high status of one who is man in a good state, and not man in a corrupted state. And so, he would achieve that he be allowed to bring out his offspring, all according to what is proper for him, in his way - meaning in the level and state that he already achieved in his being a root. And this time period was from Adam to the time of the Dispersion (after the Tower of Babel). And behold that [during] that entire time, righteous people - such as Chanokh, Metushelach, Shem and Eiver - did not stop from teaching the truth to the masses and warning them to improve themselves. But once the measure of the creatures was full - meaning at the time of the Dispersion - His trait of justice, may He be blessed, judged that the period of time for the effort of the roots end. So, it would be the end of the things that could be set according to what is proper to set at the roots, according to what already transpired and was until the time of that end. And then He, may His name be blessed, oversaw all people and saw all the levels that were fitting for these people to have set according to their deeds, and He set them on the root level, as we have explained. And according to that which they established, would be what was decreed upon them; to bring out offspring according to what was already determined to be fit for that root. And they would all be set types in the world - everyone according to his qualities and nature - like all the other species of the creations. And so, He allowed them to produce offspring according to their qualities and their character like all the other species. However, according to the Supreme Justice, they were all found to be fit to stay on the lowly level of mankind that Adam and his offspring had reached due to his sin - and not higher than this at all. And it was Abraham alone that was chosen because of his deeds. He had raised himself and was set to be an excellent and precious tree, according to the higher level of human existence, such that it was [also] given to him to produce his branches according to his qualities. And then the world was divided into seventy nations - each one of them at a certain level, but all of them in the way of mankind in its lowliness, whereas Israel was in the way of mankind in its height. And after this matter, the gate of roots was closed and the development and direction of the branches began - each one according to his character. And so, even though, prima facie, it appears that our situation now and the situation of the earlier ones is the same, in truth it is not like that. Rather until the Dispersion, it was the time of the roots of mankind, and things developed in this way. But when the end of this time period arrived, the [status of the roots] was fixed according to justice; and a new different time period began. This was the time period of the branches that we are still in now.

Abraham becoming the father of converts: Yet from His great goodness and kindness, may He be blessed, He made room even for the branches of other nations to uproot themselves from their roots, by their choice and their actions, and to include themselves in the branches of our father Abraham, peace be upon him, if they [so] desired. And this is His, may His name be blessed, making Abraham the father of converts. And He said to him (Genesis 12:3), "and all the families of the earth shall bless themselves by you."

However, if they do not make efforts about this, they will stay within their root trees, according to their natural situation.

The final judgement of the nations of the world until the giving of the Torah: And you should know that just like the collective offspring of Adam are divided into root trees, along with their branches - as we have written - so, too is each and every tree distinguished by its main branches from which all of its parts follow and divide further. In truth, the general branches of the tree of our father Abraham, peace be upon him, reached six hundred thousand - which are those that went out of Egypt and became the Israelite nation and among which the Land of Israel was divided. And all those who come after them are considered parts of these general [branches]. And it was surely to them that the Torah was given, and about them was it then said that this tree reached its time. However, the Holy One, blessed be He, did a great kindness with all of the nations, and suspended their judgement until the time of the giving of the Torah. So, He brought the Torah to all of them to accept it. And if they would have accepted it, it would still have been possible for them to raise themselves from their lowly level. But since they did not want [it], their judgement was completely finished; so, the gate was shut in front of them with a seal that cannot be opened. Yet it still remained possible for each and every individual part of the branches to convert alone, and enter by choice into the tree of our father Abraham.

The portion given to the nations of the world: Nevertheless, the decree was not to destroy these nations. Rather, the decree was that they should remain on the lowly level that we mentioned. And this is a type of man that would not be fit to exist if Adam had not sinned. Yet his sinning caused him to exist. However, since he has an aspect of man - even though he is lowly - the Holy One, blessed be He, wanted that they have that which is similar to the true mankind. And that is that they have a soul, similar to the souls of the Children of Israel, even thought its level is much lower than the level of the souls of Israel; and that they have commandments through which they also, acquire physical and spiritual success, according to that which is appropriate for their condition - and these are the Noachide laws. And note that all of the things were prepared to be like this in the case that Adam would sin - like all of the other damagers and punishments which were created conditionally, like the [Sages'] statement, may they be blessed (Avodah Zarah 5a).

What is prepared for the nations of the world in the world to come: However, nations besides Israel will not be found at all in the world to come. Existence will be given to the pious ones of the nations of the world by way of being an addition and appendage of Israel itself. And they will be secondary to them like clothing is secondary to a person. That which is coming to them from the good will come to them in this way; and it is not in their condition to attain more than this at all.

The seventy ministering angels of the nations of the world: And behold that at the time that the world was divided like this, the Holy One, blessed be He, appointed seventy officials of the angelic variety to be the appointees over these nations, to watch over them and oversee their affairs. And He, may His name be blessed, only oversees them with a general providence, whereas the minister is the one that oversees them with individual providence from the power over this that the Master, blessed be He, gave over to him. And about this thing is it stated (Amos 3:2), "You alone have I known from all the families of the earth." And, God forbid, that there be any absence of His knowledge, may He be blessed, about their details on account of this - since everything is always visible and revealed in front of Him, may He be blessed. Rather the matter is that He does not oversee and influence their particulars. And you will understand this thing in that which we will explain still further, with God's help.

Effect of the actions of the nations of the world: However, the Master, blessed be he, makes the improvement and elevation of creation dependent upon Israel, as I have written. And, as it were, He subjugates His direction to their actions - to give light and bounty; or to, God forbid, conceal Himself and hide based on their actions. However, the actions of the nations do not add or subtract from the existence of creation or from His revelation, may His name be blessed; or from His hiding. Rather they bring benefit or loss to themselves - whether for the body or for the soul - and add power to their minister or weaken him.

Providence over them: Yet even though the Holy One, blessed be He, does not oversee the nations in their details, it is already possible that He oversee them for the sake of an individual or a group of Israelites. Nevertheless this is by way of events which are a means, that we explained in the previous chapter (On Personal Providence 12).

On How Providence Works

Behold that up until now we have explained the rules of providence. Now we will speak something about the ways of providence. And this matter is divided into two parts: The first is His oversight, may He be blessed; and the second is His influence.

Regarding His providence, may He be blessed: Regarding His oversight, may He be blessed, we already know that He, may His name be blessed, knows everything, and that there is no lack of knowledge with Him at all - not in the future, not in the present and not in the past. For everything that was and will be is already seen in front of Him forever. And nothing is hidden from him, and everything is revealed in front of Him. And it is known in front of Him, may He be blessed, in all of its aspects; such that nothing is hidden from Him at all. Nevertheless, it is only said that He has oversight over things when He judges them and makes decrees that are limited by time about them, when he wants to do something new to them. And we will speak more about this further with God's help (Unit 2, The System of Providence 3).

Regarding His influence: However, His influence is that which He, may He be blessed, brings out His will to take effect in the order and calibration that He wants. It is [like] He surely ordered His creatures in an order, calibration and unfolding because He desired such an order. Just like He wanted that unfurling in the aspect of the creatures' existence, so, too did He want it in the aspect of their permanence and their actions, in all of their functions. And He preserves them in all of their aspects in this order, and influences them for what He wants about their functions and interactions. And behold He, may His name be blessed, influences an angel, and that angel influences the angel beneath him in the chain; and so, on, one level after another until the last angel acts upon the physical to preserve something or to institute it according to the transmission of the decree of His will, may He be blessed. Nevertheless, the preservation of every existing thing, at all levels, is only from Him, may He be blessed. For it is He, with His power, that preserves the creatures and their unfolding's - every one according to its function. But carrying out the actions into physicality, according to the order of the existing things and their interactions that we mentioned above, is only done through the chain that we mentioned.

The effect of the natural appointees at their posts: And behold the Master, blessed be He, put into the nature of each appointee to stand at his post and boldly fulfill what was given over into his hands. And he is not pushed off from his post except by the order that the Master, blessed be He, ordered. By way of example, the ministering angel of trees makes efforts and exerts himself to strengthen his trees. However, when there is a decree from in front of Him, may

He be blessed, the ministering angel of wind strengthens the wind according to what was decreed about it and accordingly pushes off the ministering angel of trees. So, according to this, some of his trees are uprooted from the power of the wind. And there is much calibration and great detail in these things. For there are angels that are appointed over physical nature that strengthen all parts of the physical world with their natural laws. But above them are the ministering angels of the decrees of repayment that prevent the angels of nature from effecting their functions, due to the decrees. And how many details to the details are there, according to the wonders of the secrets of His direction, may He be blessed!

Nevertheless, He, may He be blessed, oversees everything - the higher ones and the lower ones, the roots and their branches - and always aims at perfection of the collective, such that He moves all of creation towards it. And it is distributed to [individuals] according to their situation - these to be pushed off and those to be brought close; these to be purged and those to rest. Each one [receives] what is appropriate to happen to him, to bring about perfection in the general creation.

Regarding miracles: But note that He, may His name be blessed, changes the rules of creation according to His will at any time that He wants; and He does miracles and wonders with different things as He desires. [He does this,] as He decrees that it will be proper for the purpose of creation according to the situation or according to the time. So, what is this that they, may their memory be blessed, said (Genesis Rabbah 5:4), "The Holy One, blessed be He, made conditions with all of the work of creation."? It is not that the Holy One, blessed be He, would not change anything from now on. For He could certainly make a complete change any time He wants. Rather the matter is that at the time of the creation, He showed and informed all of the roots of the creatures their functions, the truth of their existence, the purpose of their creation, what they would effect in the future with their processes and what would be the end of their functions. And they grasped and knew that all was going to be for the purpose of the true good. And they accepted the thing and rejoiced in it. And this is [the meaning of] that which they, may their memory be blessed, said in a homiletical teaching, "All the works of creation were created with their consent." However, when the Holy One, blessed be He, informed them of their true function and laws and the truth of all the processes, He also, showed them that those miracles that would be performed upon them for Israel or for the righteous among them at certain times were from among the things that were needed for their perfection. Of course, this thing was [first] stated to the roots of the higher ones and afterwards unfolded down; and [then] the things were established in the physical realm as is fitting for them. And appointees were placed over them that strengthen them in their natural law. However, at the time that the Holy One, blessed be He, wants, He decrees over his appointees and they stop their assignment and change their natural process, due to the decree that was upon them. And it is actually possible that the decrees coming to them be in different ways. The explanation [of this] is that it comes - by way of example - like the command of a king or like the rebuke of a furious governor, as the matter is stated (Psalms 106:9), "And He rebuked the Red Sea, and it dried, etc." [Likewise,] that which is similar to this among the ways; everything according to the situation and its time.

On the System of Providence

Regarding the supernal courts: The Master, blessed be He, ordered that the direction of His entire world - whether that which is for the judgement of the actions of the ones with free choice or whether that which is fit to institute for the world and its creatures - would be done in an order like that of an earthly kingdom. Likewise, they, may their memory be blessed, said (Berakhot 58a), "The kingdom of the Heavens is like the kingdom of the earth." [This is to] mean courts and synods, with all of their ways and laws. And this is since He surely ordered different courts of spiritual beings of certain levels and certain orders; such that all the things that are fit to judge are placed in front of them. And according to their verdict do all the things stand, as it is written in Daniel (Daniel 4:14), "This sentence is decreed by the watchers, etc."

Judgement in the supernal court: And behold He, may His name be blessed, appears in all of these synods, and influences them and guides them to the content of the matter in truth - such that the true judgment come out. And in some of these synods, the Holy One, blessed be He, is there at the head - like the matter that is stated (I Kings 22:19), "I saw the Lord seated upon His throne, with all the host of Heaven standing in attendance to the right and to the left of Him." And they, may their memory be blessed, explained (Yerushalmi Sanhedrin 1:1), "These are going to the right for merit and those are going to the left for guilt." And Daniel said, (Daniel 7:9-10) "While thrones were set in place, and the Ancient of Days took His seat... the court sat and the books were opened."

Regarding the witnesses of the supernal court: However, the essence of the matter is like this: We have already explained above how much precision is found in the judgement of each and every individual. For behold in general with every individual, many arguments will be found according to the different causes, such that the individual can be judged in many ways. And in the particulars also, each and every one of his actions is found to have an aspect of innocence and an aspect of guilt, in many different ways. For all the matters of the world are truly combined from many combinations and lead to different ways. Nevertheless, all of these true aspects are accurately revealed in these supernal courts. And each one of the hosts that is found in that court has one aspect revealed to him according to his [own] character, until - among all of them - every aspect is revealed; not one thing is withheld. And then the matter is weighed according to all of these true aspects, such that the decree comes out according to what is proper. However, this conclusion is made by the one who is the head of that court. And if it is one of the courts that the Master, blessed be He, wants to sit at its head - note that even though everything is foreseen in front of Him, He lets all of the host of servants argue in front of Him, according to the aspect of the matter that is truly revealed to them. [Hence] the matter is concluded as it should. And it comes out according to this principle that the Holy One, blessed be He, does not judge the world from the aspect of His knowledge, but rather from the aspect of the order that He wanted to set up for the matter. And from what He further ordered is that no matter at all should be judged in any [supernal] court until appointees that He appointed for this are brought in front of Him. And this matter is that He appointed appointees of the angelic type to oversee all of the things that occur in the world. And these come to the supernal court and testify about the things that they grasped and were revealed to them, such that these matters are [all] brought to judgement. And I have already mentioned several times that these matters are not a result of His [lack of] knowledge, may He be blessed. For none of these matters are needed by Him, since everything is always foreseen by Him. Rather this is how He decreed and ordered it in His amazing wisdom. So, the world truly functions according to these arrangements. And it is about these matters that Scripture hints at in its metaphors - like the matter that is stated (Genesis 11:5), "The Lord came down to look, etc."; "and the divine beings came to present themselves, etc." (Job 1:6); "the eyes of the Lord range over the whole earth"

(Zechariah 4:10); "These were sent out by the Lord to roam the earth" (Zechariah 1:10); and others like them. It is all stated about the ways of [God's] direction according to the arrangements that He designed. And those angels appointed to oversee the affairs of the world and testify about them are called "the eyes of the Lord." And when He, may His name be blessed, reveals Himself to one of these courts to judge one of the matters - such as the builders of the Tower [of Babel] at its time, it is stated, "The Lord came down to look, etc." However, you should reflect that the comparison in these matters to that which is done in earthly kingdoms is only about the arrangements. But in the manner that the things are done, the comparison is untrue. For the physical [judges] act in accordance with what is applicable to them, in terms of what they grasp and in all their other qualities; whereas the spiritual [judges act] in accordance with what is applicable to them, in terms of what they grasp and their qualities.

Regarding the prosecutor: And note that the Master, blessed be He, put forth a prosecutor and that is the Satan - as it is stated (Job 1:6), "and the Satan also, came among them." And his appointment is to seek justice in the courts; and when he prosecutes, the judges are aroused to judge. And it is from His trait of goodness, may He be blessed, that a man not be seized in judgement until the prosecutor prosecutes - even though the sins of the sinner are revealed in front of Him. However, He even inscribed laws about this and set up arrangements - meaning how and when the prosecution of the prosecutor should be. And it is like the matter that they, may their memory be blessed, wrote (Genesis Rabbah 91:9), "The Satan prosecutes at a time of [physical] danger"; and also, what they, may their memory be blessed, wrote (Berakhot 55a), "Three things bring up the sin of a man"; and many other details similar to this.

Axioms of supernal justice: Moreover there are laws and ordered ways about all of these matters of judgement, in their generalities and in their specifics - like His Wisdom, may He be blessed, decreed about the times of judgement and their distinctions: For example, that which they, may their memory be blessed, said (Rosh Hashanah 16a), "The world is judged at four time periods" and that which they said (Rosh Hashanah 16a), "the King enters first, in order that the fury of His anger should abate." And likewise, that which they said (Rosh Hashanah 16a), "Grain is judged with two judgments"; and the differences between before the verdict and after the verdict and many other details similar to these.

On the Influence of the Stars

Behold, I have already explained in section one that all physical items have their root in transcendent powers. In truth all these items are rooted there in every necessary fashion, and only afterwards are drawn down and translated into physicality in the manner required of them. The heavenly spheres with all their stars were prepared for this purpose. Through their rotation all that is rooted and prepared above in the spiritual world is drawn down and translated into our physical world here below, set in its proper place. The number of the stars, their various levels and divisions, are set according to the highest wisdom in order to achieve this translation. The power of existence flows from the stars to every physical item below, they are the means to transform everything from its transcendent form above to its manifest form below.

There is another matter which the Holy One engraved into the stars. All the events of the physical world are prepared above and only then drawn down by the stars in they way in which they are meant to occur. For example - matters of life, wealth, wisdom, children and the like are all prepared above in the roots and made manifest below through the stars in their proper manner. Each of these happen though well-known divisions, particular groupings and known orbits assigned to them. Among all these are divided everything which occurs in the physical world. All physical matters are under their control, functioning according to the influences of their orders and connections to each and every individual.

The subjugation of the lower creatures to the influence of the stars and its nullification in the case of Israel: And note that all people are also, subjugated to this order, for things to arise for them according to what follows from the orchestration. However, it is actually possible for the effect of the stars to be nullified by a strong power above them. And based on this principle, they said (Shabbat 156a), "There is no constellation (mazal) for Israel." For the power of His decree, may He be blessed, and His influence overcome the power invested in the influence of the orchestration, such that the outcome will be according to the superior influence and not according to the influence of the orchestration.

The influence of the stars on events: Nevertheless, the [understanding of the] laws of this influence of the stars is also, limited, according to what the Supreme Wisdom decreed to be appropriate. Hence some of its ways are known according to the ways of those that observe it, and this is that which the diviners of the heavens grasp. However, not all of its true ways are revealed by this. Hence the stargazers will only grasp some of the future content of the stars - and only partially. And all the more so, when there is a nullification of their effects, as we have mentioned. And therefore they, may their memory be blessed, said (Genesis Rabbah 5:3), "'From that' (Isaiah 47:13) and not 'all of that.'"

On Specific Modes of Providence

From that which is very discernible about His providence, may He be blessed, is that the foundations of all of the arrangements of His providence are righteous law and precise justice. And [this] is like the matter that is stated (Psalms 45:7), "your royal scepter is a scepter of righteousness." And it is [likewise,] written (Proverbs 29:4), "By justice a king sustains the land." However, we know that the true desire of the Holy One, blessed be He, is only to do good. And note that He loves His creatures like a father loves his son. Yet by reason of the love itself, it is appropriate for a father to discipline his son in order to benefit him in the end - like the matter that is stated (Deuteronomy 8:5), "as like when a man disciplines his son, the Lord your God will discipline you." So, it comes out that the judgement and the verdict itself flows from a place of love; such that the discipline of the Holy One, blessed be He, is not the blow of an enemy or one taking revenge, but rather the discipline of a father that wants the good for his son, as we wrote. Indeed, there are two matters that come out of this: The first is that the discipline itself is sweetened and not harsh or cruel. For the love that is with it mixes the judgement with mercy. And the second is that sometimes when the time requires it, the Master, blessed be He, will completely pass over the letter of the law, and act with mercy. And [this is] like the matter that is stated (Exodus 33:19), "and I will have grace upon whom I will have grace, and I will have mercy upon whom I will have mercy." But behold, since the Holy One, blessed be He, wanted the free choice of man in his actions; and, according to the righteousness of His law, the reward to be paid to a man according to his deeds - He surely, as it were, subjugates His direction to the deeds of man, such that He only cause good or bad according to [man's] deeds. However, in truth, the Master, blessed be He, is surely not subjugated to any law and does not require anyone else and is not acted upon by anything. Hence when He wants to use His pre-eminence, he surely acts and directs [the world] as He wants, without any compunction or hindrance at all. However, regarding [His] normative direction, He directs [the world] according to the subjugation that we mentioned. Yet when His Wisdom decrees that it is appropriate to go beyond the letter of the law, He certainly uses His pre-eminence to pass over sin and rectify any damage with His great power. It comes out that there are two types of providence here: The providence of God, may He be blessed, and the providence of Dominion and Unity. For behold, He normally presides with normative providence, to judge all of his creation; whereas He [only occasionally] presides with the providence of Dominion to preserve the creation with His power and ability - so, that it not be destroyed by the evil acts of people.

The goodly and bad states of this world: And from that which you also, need to know is that His influence is also, surely divided into two categories: The first is that which is over the body and the second is that which is over the spirit. We have already explained the content of that which is over the body, meaning the success of man and his tranquility in this world. As to what is over the soul, it is in that which man understands, knows and draws near to Him, may He be blessed, His glory and His spiritual stature. For indeed, the goodly state in this world is truly for people to cling to wisdom and be involved in the service of their Creator, such that the truth be visible and clear, evil be oppressed and humbled, and deceit be dismissed. And [then] you shall not find any worship in the world except for that to Him, may He be blessed. And all of the good traits will be found; and all of the bad traits will be rejected. And corresponding to this, tranquility and peace will grow, and afflictions and hurts not be found. And the Master, blessed be He, will have His glory dwell openly in His world and be glad about His creatures and His creations. And His creations will be happy and joyful in front of Him. And the opposite of this will be if people are drowning in their desire, rejecting wisdom and [staying] far from it; and only a few or none are turning to [divine] service. So, the truth will [fall] to the earth, evil will become strong, deceit and error will be great, foreign worship will be in the world, the good traits will disappear and all of the bad traits will be very common. And corresponding to this will peace be missing and there will be no tranquility. Likewise, will there be afflictions and many injuries. So, the Master, blessed be He, will hide His glory from His world; and the world will continue as if it were left to happenstance and given over to nature. And the Holy One, blessed be He, will not be happy about His creatures and people will not be happy in front of Him. And they will not [even] recognize and know what joy of the creatures in front of their Creator is. And at such a time, the evil ones will dominate and the good ones will be demeaned. So, it comes out that all is influenced from Him, may He be blessed - those matters relevant to the body in those parts of the situation that we mentioned; and those matters that are relevant to the spirit.

The influence of the emanation of His countenance and the influence of the hiding of His countenance: Behold it has already been explained in Part I, Chapter 4 (On Human

Responsibility 3) that the state of man in this world is indeed physical, that darkness is rooted within him, and that emanation - from which he gets intellect and spirit - is combined and associated with it. And note that at the beginning of man's formation, his foolishness is great and his intellect is meager. But as a youth grows, his intellect matures. However, the cause of all of these realities is His influence, may He be blessed. For a man's existence and content will be according to what He influences - in general and specifically. And the root of all this is the matter of the emanation of His presence or its hiding that we explained above in Part I, Chapter 4 (On Human Responsibility 10) - which is the root of the existence of good and evil everywhere that they are. Behold that influence comes from the emanation of His presence or His hiding it, according to what the Supreme Wisdom decrees. From the influence of its emanation there comes bounty, clarity and preciousness. And from the influence of its hiding comes lack, heaviness and lowliness. And since the existence of things and their proper direction requires the combination of these things in strong association - for in one very item, and in that which is fitting to be in it, there are elements of lack in one aspect and elements of bounty in another aspect; elements of heaviness and elements of clarity; elements of lowliness and elements of preciousness - the influence that must therefore be imposed upon them must be a combination of emanation and hiding according to what is appropriate to come out in those influenced. And according to what is rooted in it, and according to the order that is arranged and the gradation in which the elements are rooted in their influence, so, will its results come out in all of their aspects and demarcations. And this is a great principle about all of existence and occurrences in every place that they may be.

The fourth level of the state of the world: When we observe the general conditions of the world since it was created, according to the events that have happened in it and that which the prophets have reported about them - it comes out that there is a four-fold gradation in the matter. We can think of it as if all of the human specie were one man from the time of his birth to his fully coming of age. And behold that the first state is one in which foolishness and darkness is highly dominant, such that true knowledge of the Creator, may He be blessed, and His perfection are greatly lacking. And that is what the Sages, of blessed memory, called the two thousand [years] of void. The second state is a better one than that which we mentioned, and it is like the state of our times. For we surely have - praise to God - knowledge of God's existence, may He be blessed, and His perfection; the Torah of the Lord is with us and we worship Him. However, there is no sign or prophet; and true understanding - which is the holy spirit (ruach hakodesh) - is lacking. For, in fact, that which a man understands according to his intellect through human effort in comparison with that which he understands with the spirit of a [divinely] influenced intellect is like the comparison of a mere body to [its] soul. The third state, which is better than this, is like the state of the time of the Temple in which there were already signs, wonders and prophecy among the human species. However, this influence is only found spread to individuals and not to all, as there is an obstacle and hindrance to the matter. The fourth state is better than all of them, and it is what the prophets report about in the future to come. [In it,] there will be no foolishness at all and the holy spirit will pour forth upon the entire human specie without difficulty at all. And then it will surely be said that the development of the human specie has been completed. For from then onward, they will be prodigious and enjoy [this state] for ever and ever.

The limits of spiritual influence: And concerning the spiritual influence that we mentioned, there are other demarcations with respect to time, place and other conditions. For the Master, blessed be He, inscribed and set up that He would be present and revealed at certain times and in specific ways, beyond how He is revealed at other times; likewise, [to be revealed] in a place beyond how He is revealed in other places. And all of this is with many distinctions and details which are determined with great precision, according to that which is appropriate for the refinement of the creatures. And upon this is the holiness of days and holy places dependent, such that people can attain greater influence and receive emanation, clarity and stature in conjunction with the determined gradation.

Part Three

On the Soul and Its Activities

Regarding the speaking spirit: Behold the makeup of man which is not found in any other creature has already been explained in Part I, Chapter 3 (On Mankind 2) - meaning the combination of two disparate and distinct realities that are combined in him, the body and the soul. And this is because there is the existence of a spirit in man which serves for feeling and understanding embedded in his nature - like there is in every animal. And the matter of this spirit in all the animals is an element that is very fine, that comes from the seed after conception. And it is what spreads, grows and builds the body according to what is fitting for that species. It likewise, spreads with it, when it grows; and the feeling and understanding appropriate for that specie is dependent upon it. For note that there are great distinctions in understanding even among the animals themselves. But the understanding of humans is very different than the understanding of all of them. However, all of this occurs in the spirit, according to the laws of nature and according to the formation of the vessels that serve it in each and every specie, based on what it is. Yet the spirit of man is distinguished by [various] facets and powers - such as imagination, memory, intellect and will.

All of these are powers of the spirit, demarcated by clear demarcations and functioning in specific ways.

Regarding the separate spirit: However, besides all of this, there is also, a separate and highly elevated spiritual element found in man. And its only purpose in coming into man is to connect him to the higher roots, with which he must connect in order for his deeds have an impact on the higher powers. And in this situation, the influence comes to man from the higher sources, and from it to the spirit that we mentioned [previously to this], and from it to the body. So, the higher spirit directs the lower one and effects it with all the needed effects for the various times of a man, according to its relation and connection with the higher forces. And behold that that spirit is connected to the lower one, and the lower to the finest portion of the blood. So, it comes out that the body and the two souls are all connected with each other.

The effect of the separate spirit on the body and the body's effect on it: And behold because of this connection though which this spirit is connected with the body via the lower spirit, it is limited in specific ways. So, combination and involvement with the spiritual and ethereal essences are prevented the whole time it is connected with the body - meaning all of the days of a man's life. [Rather,] it is affected by the actions of the body, to be associated through them with the light of the Creator, blessed be He; or to veer away from Him and to cling to the forces of impurity. And preparation for [the ideally] destined perfection, or the distancing from it, is dependent upon this. It also, impacts upon the man: It directs the lower soul, guides it and engraves the outlines of understanding, according to its preparation. And it brings out thoughts and the will according to the direction in which it veers.

The distinguishable parts in the aggregate soul and their proceedings: However, even though we more generally called it one spirit, see that it is actually made up of many parts and various levels. And we could even say that there are many spirits that are interconnected like the rings of a chain. So, just like a chain is built, as befits it, from all of [the rings], so, too is the aggregate higher spirit that we mentioned built from all of these spiritual levels. And they are all interconnected, with the last one connected to the lower spirit and the lower spirit connected to the blood, as we have written. And it is even possible for some of these parts to withdraw at a certain time and return later, or for levels to be added and then later go away. And no trace of all this is seen in the body at all. For these spiritual actions are not at all felt in the body - such that they add or take away anything from life, or in something that is felt. Rather their functions concern that which man really is and his relationship to the higher roots, according to how it is fit for him to be connected to them. Behold that included in this is the matter of the extra soul that comes on the holy Shabbat and leaves at the conclusion of Shabbat, yet its coming and going is not felt by the body. And behold the aggregate soul is divided into five parts; and they are called the spirit (nefesh), the essence (ruach), the soul (neshema), the life (chayah) and the singularity (yechidah).

Regarding "his constellation saw": Yet this higher soul is subject to unique experiences, appropriate for it according to its nature. Even though it is connected to the body, as we have written, it retains some commonality with the spiritual - to the extent that it is not prevented by its connection to the body. Nevertheless, nothing is felt and recognized by man's intellect and mind, except occasionally. And this is that which they, may their memory be blessed, said, "He did not see, but his constellation saw" (Megillah 3a) - that the matter already comes to this higher spirit; yet a full image does not come to the mind and the intellect, but rather only a small arousal and nothing more.

Regarding dreams: Moreover, the Supreme Wisdom saw fit to divide time into two parts. One is for the creatures to act, and the other is for their rest - and that is day and night. For daytime is the time for action and nighttime is the time for rest. And It placed into the nature of animals that they would sleep in order that there be rest for them and their spirits from their toil. And at that time, their essences reinvigorate their strength in all parts of their bodies and their spirits, so, that they return renewed in the morning for their work as at the beginning. And note that when man sleeps, his faculties rest and his emotions are quiet; and his intellect also, rests and is quiet. Only his imagination is active and goes and imagines and creates content according to what comes to it from the remnant of what he depicts during the time he is awake and from what comes to it from the vapors and gases that go up to his brain - whether from the natural humors or whether from foods. And this is the matter of everyone's dreams. But the Creator, may He be blessed, also, embedded into it that the higher spirit that we mentioned slightly remove itself at this time from its physical connections at this time. So, portions of itself - down to the essence - arise and separate from the body. And only one part - which is the spirit - remains with the lower spirit. And behold, the separated portions float, according to what is allowed them, and encounter and interact with spiritual entities - whether with supervisors of nature or with angels of prophetic reception or with demons, according to what comes to it from one of the various causes. And sometimes the content that it grasps is drawn down and unfolds to the lower spirit, such that an image is aroused and creates content according to its ways. Yet it is possible that the content that it grasps be true or false, due to the intermediaries through which it grasped it. And this content itself is drawn down to the imagination: Sometimes it is conceived of with great confusion, and much jumbling with the empty images that are drawn from the vapors; though sometimes it is with great clarity. And even information and foreknowledge about what will happen to a man in the future can reach him in these ways. And this happens according to His decree, may He be blessed, such that He informs the soul through one of His servants of any given type, and the content gets to the spirit in its imagination - either obscurely or clearly, based on what is decreed by the Supreme Wisdom. And about this matter is it stated (Job 33:15-16), "In a vision of a dream at night, etc... He then opens the ear of people." It comes out that dreams of imaginative content are either from [the imagination] itself or from that which is aroused by the soul according to that which it grasps. However, in all [of the latter], the action is only from one of the spiritual forces that informs the soul. Then the soul brings it down to the imagination, as we have written. And if the force is from the holy servants, the thing will be true; whereas if it is from the opposite forces, the matter will be false. And this is what is written (Berakhot 55b), "Here it was through an angel, but there it was through a demon." But all of them contain some mixture of empty images that are only from the imagination. And that is what is written (Berakhot 55a), "It is impossible for a dream to be without idle things." However, there are other dreams that exist, and they are prophetic dreams. And we will explain their content in a separate [section] with God's help.

On Divine Names and Witchcraft

Two levels of powers: We have already explained in the previous sections that the origin of all the creatures is the aggregate of all the ethereal forces arranged in a certain order with well-known divisions; and they unfold from them in the gradation of physical entities according to their species. We also, explained the matter of the powers of evil, from which all of the physical evils unfold. We also, explained that the main essence of that which is created is the ethereal roots; and that that which is physical is only an extension of what is rooted and established there. And it is there that what is fitting to be extended is arranged and extended according to the true essence of their existence - and their content according to what is fitting to be in their roots and in their branches. So, the Supreme Wisdom extended the things with an unfolding that extends and moves content from one form to another until they are connected and limited by this physical form. And above all the physical things is their chain of roots - one above the other - until the first forces. And each one stands in its place, and exists on its level and within its boundaries that the Creator, may He bless, designed for it, such that it does not leave them. And all of the roots influence their branches according to the unfolding, without their having to leave their natural boundaries at all.

Nevertheless, the Supreme Wisdom decreed that there also, be another existence to the forces that impact on the physical, which is not according to the order of unfolding. And that is that they themselves act upon the physical entities, and they relate to their laws and not to those of the physical. And these are actions of theirs through which they change physical entities from their usual nature. And so, man was given the ability to use entities in this way, just as he was given the ability to use them in the natural way; and in the very same manner that use was given to him in the natural [way]. The explanation [of this] is that just like the use of nature is not completely according to his will, but he is only able to use it according to well-known ways and within specific limits - as he may surely only cut with a knife and that which is similar to it, and he can only climb up with a ladder, and he can only squash something soft and all that is similar to this - so, too is the spiritual use [of things] only given to him according to certain well-known limits and specific ways, according to that which the Divine Wisdom saw to be appropriate.

That a man can somewhat develop away from physicality: And also, part of this matter is because of that which we already explained that man is a combination of two opposites - the body and the soul - such that the soul is limited and bound by the axioms that are connected to it according to what the Supreme Wisdom decreed about it. So, man is limited in his embodied condition by the axioms of the body and the properties of the material; and the soul is bound by these chains, it cannot escape from them. However, the Master, blessed be He, desired that there be a way for man to be able to release himself a little from these physical limits and their unfolding, and to reach matters that are not according to the axioms of the physical, but rather like the axioms of the spiritual. And through this, he can reach an understanding of the spiritual entities and their properties, which would have been prevented from him according to his physical condition and its limits. Then he is accordingly more able to bring all of existence to the condition that is good and proper for it - above and below, in the roots and in the branches.

And behold the Supreme Wisdom set up that there be a suspension of some of the natural limits of the material and of this world, that separate and distance man from the spiritual entities and their content, that man be freed from their bounds and that he stand on a more elevated level than his physical level; such that he was given a connection and common ground with the spiritual entities even while he is in this world in his darkened body. However, not all of the natural limits were designed to be annulled, but rather only some of them that the Supreme Wisdom saw to be appropriate for the general intention of [His] direction, as we wrote in Part I. And even these [that are annulled] are only [annulled] with great precision, according to designated conditions and well-known ways

Means through which a man can develop away from physicality: Truly, His Wisdom, may He be blessed, set up means through which a man is able to attain this goal if he wants and make efforts through them. [The goal] being the annulment of these natural limits from him and his placing himself in the state that we mentioned. And all of their content is dependent upon that which I will now explain: Regarding His names, may He be blessed, and making use of them: You should know that it has been explained that the Master, blessed be He, is the existence of all things - both in their general qualities and in their particulars. So, it comes out that all entities and their arrangements - the higher powers, the spiritual creations and the physical creations - only exist by that which He, may His name be blessed, exists for them to depend upon. So, behold He exists and reveals Himself to all that He makes exist, and influences them according to what is fitting for them to preserve their makeup. Hence there are many and diverse influences that are found, according to the multiplicity of receivers and their differences. And the existence of all that exists and their divisions and makeups is dependent upon these influences. And when these influences are brought down, effects are produced that bring about their impact that comes about through all of the unfolding, that exists according to that which He set up. And so, the angels receive some of His light, may He be blessed, which reveals to them what they receive, and the higher creatures [transmit this further] to the lower creatures until the end of all of the unfolding. Yet He, may His name be blessed, wanted to be called by name, in order that His creatures could be aroused towards Him and call Him, to mention Him and to come closer to Him. It is true that He selected the explicit name (the tetragrammaton) for His glory, and said about it (Exodus 3:15), "this is My name forever, etc." And this is the name that He is called based on the glory itself, according to what He wanted to be called by name. However, in accordance with all of the specific influences, He [also] wanted to be called by several names. So, He decreed and embedded that when His creatures mention [one of] His name[s], emanation and influence would be brought down. And [it is] like the matter that is stated (Exodus 20:21), "in every place that I will cause My name to be mentioned, I will come to you and bless you." Truly, it is according to the name that they mention and with which they call, that the influence is brought down through that mention. The explanation [of this] is that the influence that is brought down will be that type of influence the secret of which He, may He be blessed, associated with this name. In fact, in the bringing down of the influence, the embedded effect will forcibly come about and the content will extend through all of its unfolding from the top to the bottom, as we have written. As behold, the Supreme Wisdom limited the content with given limits and specific conditions, such that when its mention is carried out, that influence - and none else - is affected, and its impact is made. And see that among these influences that He decreed that would be brought down from Him, may He be blessed, He set up influences that when they come down and reach the one who receives them, annul some of the limits of nature, as we wrote. So, this person will connect with spiritual beings and attain knowledge and understanding above human understanding, as well as other things that are branches of this root. And this is the matter of the holy spirit and of prophecy, as we will discuss more later with God's help. And behold, He decreed that the bringing down of these influences also, be through the means that we mentioned - meaning, His names, may He be blessed, that He associated with these influences - with the concentration of heartfelt thought or by mentioning them orally or combined with things that are conditions for what is required to be joined to this, and as we will further discuss with God's help.

And behold it is a well-known thing that even though this general principle is one matter - meaning, the overriding of natural limits - the details of the matter are many, according to the arrangements of existence, [its] entities and their levels. For according to that which is given by the nature of the entities and their arrangements, so, will be the details of the influences needed to execute the thing in all of its aspects. According to this, the details of the mentioning and its conditions become many. And in this overriding, itself, that we mentioned, there are many, many levels - as with all other general categories divided into specifics. So, there will be one who overrides a little of [his physical] connections and limits, and one who overrides a little more. And we will speak more about this further with God's help.

It is truly upon this foundation that man's ability to manipulate [higher] entities by way of spiritual manipulation exists, as we wrote above. [It is also, the basis for his] performing great and powerful deeds, which are not possible through the manipulation of the physical. And that is because the Master, blessed be He, surely set up the arrangements of existence and their tracks according to this way, such that they are interconnected with one another - and all of them are dependent upon His influences that we mentioned, may He be blessed, in the following way: When you bring down one of the influences by mentioning of one of His names, may He be blessed - as we mentioned - this brings about an effect through to the end of its unfolding. For see that He, may His name be blessed, makes available for those who call Him with this name that which He arranged and wanted that it light up that light and provide that influence upon which the existence of that desired matter is dependent through to the end of the matter in physicality. But there is another matter that the Creator, may His Name be blessed, embedded in this way. And that is since all of the angels in all of their levels have the power to do the deeds that were given over to them. But behold it is not that they act all the time, but rather according to the order that was arranged for the constant natural direction of the world. However, they [also] have in their power, to be able to act with a certain action that is more than what they regularly do, and with more power and strength - not like the regular order. And they often act in this way in the production of miracles and wonders that occur in the world according to His will, may He be blessed, at the time that He wants. Nevertheless the Master, blessed be He, wanted to give glory to His name, such that if it be mentioned over the angels according to the order that He arranged - meaning over an angel with a specific action, the name that He, may He be blessed, associated with that influence upon which that matter completely depends - that angel is surely coerced to act with that extra power that is given to him for that action, according to what the one who mentions the name upon him coerces him [to do]. So, it comes out that there are two roots in this matter. The first one is the mentioning of His name, may He be blessed - like one who calls to Him to answer him. And through this, he brings down the influence, through which various things will come about. The second one is that he will coerce the angels through His name, may He be blessed, to act with an action that is more than what they constantly do. Of course, neither of these things are completely determined by the will of the person. Rather they are limited by limitations and conditions; and circumscribed by the extent to which this ability can be used and the manner in which it will succeed. And it is always possible that the effect will be prevented and the action hindered, even within the actual extent that is given for it to work - just like an effect of the manipulation of nature can also, be prevented by His, decree, may He be blessed, if He decrees about it. Regardless, the first root - which is mentioning His name, may He be blessed, to bring down influence through it - certainly requires closeness to Him, may He be blessed, and cleaving to Him. And the more that the one doing it increases this quality, the more the thing will succeed in his hands. And the more that he lacks it, the more difficult reaching the goal will be for him. But with the second root, this condition is not necessary - even if it is not prevented from helping him, if he has it. For behold, once the mystical power was put into these names to coerce the angels when they are mentioned, they surely came to be like any other natural tool - that the one who uses it can do so, according to his will, so, long as he uses it in the correct way. That said, it is obvious that it is not fitting or proper for a commoner to use the 'scepter of the King.' And about this thing, they, may their memory be blessed, said (Avot 1:13) "one who makes [unworthy] use of the crown shall pass away." And the only dispensation for the thing is for the holy ones and for the ones close to Him, may He be blessed, to use this for something that will bring about a sanctification of His name, may He be blessed, and the accomplishment of His will in some way. And even though the action will not be prevented to the user if he correctly observes the methods of its use, he will certainly be punished for his wantonness. And I have already said that the matter is not completely determined [by human action], but rather limited with limitations which the Supreme Wisdom saw fit to be appropriate. And even within that limit itself, His decree, may He blessed, can prevent the effect anytime He desires, when its stopping is appropriate and proper.

Regarding "and also, this one across from that one did God make": And behold since the Supreme Wisdom decreed that there be good and evil in the world, the arrangement should be that evil truly be found in all the levels in which it is possible to be found, such that man's work be to prevent its domination and activity in all of its ways and levels until its presence be completely removed from all of creation. Of course, you see that the truth of the nature of the Master, blessed be He, is that He is devoid of any type of lack that there may be, as we have written in Part I, Chapter 1 (On the Creator 2). It is only in the creatures that is possible for there to be lacking and evil. So, the arrangement was truly that levels of good be created for the creatures and that its opposite - which is evil - [also] be created for them. This was the bringing about of that which can be evil. And man would come through his service and remove its content completely and establish good in himself and in the creation for ever and ever. And hence the arrangement was that for every good thing, there be found an evil thing corresponding to it. And this is that which the verse states (Ecclesiastes 7:14), "and also, this one across from that one did God make." And there is only one thing in which good has an advantage over evil: That the root of good is God's primordial and everlasting perfection, whereas evil is something created only in order to nullify it. And its only use is during the time of man's effort that we mentioned above.

Regarding sorcery: And so, in this way, just as He brought about a way for man to acquire emanation, understanding and the holy spirit in a supernatural way beyond the physical; so, too was it necessary to bring about the opposite of this great good, such that man could bring down darkness, murkiness and a spirit of impurity in a supernatural way. And this is the matter of the impurities of sorcery and the seeking out of the dead from which the Torah distanced us. And its content is the bringing down of the influences of impurity and pollution by the mentioning of words under given conditions - which is really the greatest distancing from Him, may He be blessed, [and] truly the opposite of cleaving to Him. And the thing is brought down from those forces of evil that we mentioned in Part I, Chapter 5 (On the Spiritual Realm 8), upon which He, may He be blessed, decreed names through which given levels of impurity would be brought down in a supernatural way. Accordingly, supernatural acts can be done through them, like the acts of the [Egyptian] magicians and others, according to what is placed into their hand to act within the limits that were placed upon them. Likewise, can they do acts like this through demons, according to what is given to them within the specific limits governing them. And so, - within the measure allowed by their ability to act - the Master blessed be He, decreed that they push away the appointees over nature that preserve the matters of the world in their natural state and all of the angels that bring influences according to the arranged order. And about them, they, may their memory be blessed, said (Chullin 7b), "Keshafim (Sorcery)? It is [an acronym for] makhchishin pamalya shel ma'alah (they diminish the heavenly entourage)." However, that is only within that measure and no more. And even within that measure, it is yet possible that they be pushed off by a force more powerful than them, and that their action be prevented by His decree, may He be blessed. And about this they said, "There is none like Him, and even [in the case of] sorcery." And they explained that this is for [a person] who has great merit, such that they will save him and push off those who want to do bad to him, from the Heavens. And this is what is written, "Rabbi Ḥannina is different, because his merit is great."

On Divine Inspiration and Prophecy

Regarding holy spirit (divine inspiration): Behold that the Creator, may He be blessed, implanted into man's nature that he can learn, understand and be enlightened by observing [various] entities and their characteristics. And from what is revealed in front of him, he can contemplate and deduce that which is not revealed - until he grasps it and masters it. And this is the natural way of comprehension. However, He also, decreed that there be another type of comprehension that is much superior to this. And that is the comprehension that is [divinely] inspired: That is that an influence from Him, may He blessed, comes to one through certain means that He set up for this. And when this influence reaches his intellect, clear knowledge of a certain thing is implanted in it. So, he will know the thing completely, [along] with its causes and its outcomes - everything according to its level. And this matter is called holy spirit.

Things grasped by holy spirit: And note that in this way, one may grasp matters that are within the category of natural comprehension - just with greater clarity, as we have written. But he can also, grasp matters that are not in the category of what can be grasped by natural comprehension. Included in those things are future events and hidden matters.

Sparking of holy spirit in its absence: However,, there are different levels found in the thing - in the matter of the power of the flow of the influences, in the way that it comes to a man and in the nature of the things that are revealed and made known through it. Yet in all of them, the influence exists in such a way that the one influenced is fully aware of it. However, it can also, happen that an influence will flow into the heart of a man, such that he will master the content of a certain matter but will not feel from it that he is influenced, but rather feel like someone who had a thought occur to him. And sometimes - in the words of the Sages, may their memory be blessed - this is [also] called the holy spirit, or hidden influence, by way of extension. Nevertheless, true holy spirit is clearly recognizable and felt by its holder.

Regarding prophecy: Yet there is another level above all of this, and that is prophecy. And its content is that a man reaches to connect with the Creator, may His name be blessed, and truly cleave to Him in such a way that he feels the cleaving, and grasps that to which he is cleaving - meaning to His glory, may He be blessed - according to the way we shall explain below. And the thing is clear and perceived by him without any doubt, in the same way that he would have no doubts about something physical that he perceives with his senses. Note that the essence of prophecy is the attainment of this cleaving and connection while he is still alive, which is certainly a great perfection. However, accompanying this is [also] information and understandings. For through this, he is truly able to grasp very great and true matters from His hidden secrets, may He be blessed. And he grasps them with clarity through the path of influenced understanding that we mentioned - with greater power than someone who is in possession of the holy spirit, as we will still discuss with God's help.

The manner of prophetic perception: Regardless, the manner of this perception is that it be through an intermediary - since man is not able to cleave to, or to grasp, His glory, may He be blessed, in the way one sees his fellow in front of him. Rather it is through servants that serve for [this type of] perception - like eyeglasses serve for the eye, such that it is grasped through them. However, what they actually perceive is the glory and [nothing] else. Yet the perception changes according to the difference in the intermediaries - like vision through a lens, such that there are distinguishable levels of distance and closeness, and clarity and murkiness in the various lenses.

The nature of prophesying: Behold that when He, may He be blessed, reveals Himself to the prophet and places His influence upon him, [the prophet] is greatly overpowered - such that his mass and all the limbs of his body tremble and seem like they are breaking apart. For it is an axiom of matter that it cannot tolerate the revelation of spiritual beings, all the more so, revelations of His glory, may He be blessed. And see that [the prophet's] perceptions are nullified; and even his intellectual functions do not function independently at all. Rather they all remain dependent upon Him, may He be blessed, and are brought under His influence. And observe, it is on account of his cleaving in which his soul is engaged, that a way of understanding is added to him - completely outside of all the boundaries of human understanding. For this understanding does not come from itself, but rather from its root of the Highest connecting with it. And then what it perceives will be in a more sublime manner than what it perceives on its own. And it is in this that the power of the prophet is greater than that of someone in possession of the holy spirit, even in grasping knowledge. For behold, he perceives [things] with a higher understanding than all of the understanding possible for a man - and that is understanding from the aspect of being connected to his Creator. But behold the revelation of His glory is the actor in all that is brought down to the prophet in his prophecy. And so, it is brought down through the power of imagination in the prophet's spirit - such that certain illustrated matters are forced upon him from the power of the Most High's revelation, and not from himself at all. And from these visions comes thought and understanding that is embedded from the force that reveals itself. And the matter remains fixed in his intellect, such that even when he returns to his regular human state, the clear knowledge will still be found with him. This is the general principle about the matter of prophecy among all prophets. But the details of the levels are many, as we will write about further with God's help. And above all of them is the level of our teacher Moses, peace be upon him, about whom the Torah testified (Deuteronomy 34:10), "And no other prophet arose in Israel like Moses, who knew the Lord face to face."

On the Prophetic Experience

The prophet grasps all the matters that he prophesies without a doubt: Behold that when a prophet reaches the level of full prophecy, he grasps all that comes to him with clear perception and full knowledge. The explanation of this is that even though, according to the gradation that we mentioned in the previous chapter, visions come first and it [only] reaches his thought - in the ways we mentioned - afterwards; see that when his prophecy does come to him with clarity, he will grasp that he is a true prophet. The explanation of this is that when he is connected to Him, may He be blessed - in His, may be blessed, revealing Himself to him and being the Actor behind all these actions in him; and in his grasping that the visions that are being illustrated for him are prophetic visions orchestrated by His influence, may He be blessed, upon him; and in the knowledge that comes from this influence being implanted in him - no doubt remains with him, not about his prophecy nor about any of its aspects, neither the previous ones, nor the current ones.

Regarding those learning prophecies: And among that which you need to know is that a prophet surely does not reach the highest level all at once. Rather he climbs level by level, until he reaches complete prophecy. And there is learning in this thing, like in all the other disciplines and crafts in which a man moves up in stages, until he masters it clearly. And this is the matter of the 'sons of the prophets' that would be found in front of prophets to learn what was necessary about the ways of prophecy.

Unrecognized prophecy: But note that it is possible that a revelation come from Him, may He be blessed, and that one not recognize it as a prophet would recognize it, but rather think of it [as coming from] a perceivable source - until the prophetic influence [later] overpower him, and he then recognize the matter for what it truly was. And God's call to

Samuel (I Samuel 3) was of this type: He did not prophesy at first nor did the [divine] influence come upon him. Rather a voice like a perceivable voice was revealed to him, and he did not grasp anything more. But later the influence came upon him and he recognized and grasped the prophecy and its ways. And likewise, the vision of the bush to Moses (Exodus 3) at the beginning was only revealed as something perceivable. So, he saw the bush burning in flames, and the Holy One, blessed be He, called him with the voice of his father. But afterwards, He brought the influence upon [Moses] and he grasped the truth of the prophecy.

The teaching to those learning: Indeed, the prophecy students would study given topics [about] what would bring down the influence of the Most High; how one would nullify any barriers from the material body and bring about the revelation of His light, may He be blessed and the cleaving to Him; and more generally, the mention of holy names, praises that would be joined with names in the ways of combination, as we wrote earlier. And according to that which they merited with their deeds, purified themselves and pursued these matters, they drew themselves closer to Him, may He be blessed; and began to draw the [divine] influence upon themselves. Then they reached various accomplishments until they arrived at prophecy. And an established prophet who already and expertly knew the ways of prophecy would teach them - each one according to his readiness - what to do to attain the desired goal. And likewise, when the revelations would begin to come to them, the prophet would teach them about the revelation they received and what was still lacking from the goal that they were seeking. So, they would surely require the teacher and guide, until it was clear that they completely mastered prophecy. For even though they had already begun with revelations and the influence had descended upon them - this would not be enough for them to reach the end of the matter immediately. Rather they required much guidance to reach the end properly - each one according to his level and his preparedness.

The difference among prophets: However, even after they reached the level of prophecy, the prophets were distinguished from one another in their stature and level - both quantitatively and qualitatively. The explanation of this is that there are some that would prophesy many times; whereas there are some that would only prophesy a little. And likewise, regarding the quality of the prophecy itself - there are some that would reach great cleaving with Him, may He be blessed, and arrive at very great understandings; whereas there are some for whom neither their cleaving nor their understanding would be so, [great]. Nevertheless, all those that prophesy will be equal in that their cleaving to Him, may He be blessed, will be perceivable to them; and the revelation from Him, may He be blessed, will be clear to them, with a clarity about which they have no doubt. However, they are differentiated by many levels regarding their cleaving, the revelation they receive and their understanding.

Derech Part Three Hashem

The missions of the prophets: And among that which happens to the prophets is being sent upon His missions, may He be blessed. But [it only sometimes happens,] as this is not the essence of prophecy; and it is not necessary at all for a prophet to be sent to others. Rather we have already explained that the essence of prophecy is cleaving to Him, may He be blessed, and His revelation to him, and that it is accompanied by knowledge and understandings. And it is [only one of] the events that frequently happens to prophets, that they be sent to others. And it is truly possible that this comes to a prophet that is very established in the ways of prophecy and knows them well. But it also, possible that it comes to someone who is not so, established and learned about this. And from this angle, it is possible that mistakes would occur to prophets - not in what they prophesied, but rather in that which they would do on their own, and not fulfill that which was appropriate for them to do on their mission. Hence, they were punished. And this is like the story of Jeroboam's prophet who transgressed his own words (I Kings 13). And it came to him from not being exacting in the ways of prophecy, as they, may their memory be blessed, wrote in the Talmud (Sanhedrin 89b).

It is possible for a prophet to miss something included in his prophecy, but it is impossible for him to imagine that which was not [part of] it: Behold it is also, possible that one of the prophets will grasp something true in his prophecy, but will not grasp all of the true things included in it. For example, [regarding] the prophecy of Jonah the son of Amittai, to whom it was stated (Jonah 3:4), "and Nineveh will be overturned" - two [possibly] true understandings were included in this statement: The first was that it was the punishment destined for them according to their sin; and the second was that what would [actually] happen to them was foreseen in front of Him, may He blessed - that is that they would overturn themselves from bad to good. However, if only the matter of the punishment had been truly included in the statement, once the Holy One, blessed be He, came back and regretted the [punishment], He would have revealed the thing to the prophets, and especially to Jonah - that a new decree had come out besides the first one. But since the Holy One, blessed be He, truly included both understandings in the first statement, He did not need to make a new decree for them. Rather the statement would stand according to the second understanding, and not the first. However, at the beginning, Jonah only grasped the first [understanding], and not the second. And this is what they, may their memory be blessed, said (Sanhedrin 89b), "It is Jonah that did not comprehend."

Regarding prophecy, its words and its acts: Yet you should know that there are two characteristics regarding the prophecy of those that prophesied: The first is the content and the second is the phrasing and the words. And that is because there are surely cases in which the prophet grasps content, but he is not restricted in the words; such that the prophet can say it with the words that he wants. But there are other cases in which they grasp content that that is also, restricted by words, such as the prophecies of Isaiah, Jeremiah and the other prophets that were written for [all] the generations. Those were restricted in their prophetic words to include many [simultaneous meanings]. And even in this, the metaphor varied according to the prophet's own understanding and his ways; and it even varies according to the nature of his language and his way of speaking. And frequently, prophets were given to do actions alongside their prophecies, such as Jeremiah with his belt (Jeremiah 13) and with his yoke (Jeremiah 27), Ezekiel with his brick (Ezekiel 4) and many others like those. And the content of this was that through these actions, they would arouse the higher powers that were required according to the true essence of what the prophecy - in all of its facets - was about. And then they would be prepared and stored to bring the thing out to be actualized at the time that was fit for it.

[Inexact] use of the title, prophet: You should also, know that the true and exact title, prophet, is surely only fitting for one who has already achieved clear prophecy, and to whom it is clear that he is prophesying from [God], may He be blessed, as we wrote earlier. And with one who has reached this, he has no doubt at all about his prophecy and no error will be found in his prophecy. However, by way of extension, this title is also, given to one who begins with prophetic experiences and attains revelations that are beyond what is [naturally] human. Yet one who has only reached these achievements is not yet sure of his content. So, it is possible that he will fail, like the matter of Ahab's prophets which we will explain further with God's help. Still, those who clearly know the ways of prophecy know all of this well [and] know all of these stumbling blocks that may occur. [They] know their signs and the way to avoid them, until they reach true prophecy. And they would teach the students - as we wrote above - save them from mistakes and [help] them arrive at the truth.

Regarding the false prophets: However, the essence of this matter is that which we wrote in Part I, Chapter 5 (On the Spiritual Realm 8) about those powers of impurity that exist in the world and which work according to that which is embedded in their natures and given over into their hands. And behold they have the power to fool people to bring down influences on people in ways similar to the ways of true prophecy and reveal true and false things to them. And some wondrous things will happen for him [in this way], as it is written in Scripture explicitly about the false prophet (Deuteronomy 13:2-3), "and he gives you a sign or a wonder. And the sign or wonder happens." And note that it is possible for this thing to happen to a person without willing it, and it is possible that it happens to a person willfully. This means that it is possible that this thing happens to him when he did not make efforts towards it or [even] when he made efforts towards its opposite; but it came to him [regardless], because he had not perfected his deeds and his efforts. But it is [also] possible that he wants it and evilly makes efforts to attain it. This means that he follows these powers and makes efforts to cleave to them, due to his desire to attain that which he wants to attain from them - meaning that matters be revealed to him, as we mentioned; so, that through them he can hold himself up to be a prophet in front of people and mislead them as he desires or become honored in their eyes. And of this type were the prophets of Ba'al and Asheirah. For see that they made efforts towards this until they were cleaving to those powers and attained some knowledge of things - through which they would seduce those who believed them - and also, bring forth wonders through this power, as a sign of their being prophets. But they themselves would know that this only came to them from the angle of the impurity they had chosen for themselves. So, they themselves did not think they were prophets, but did it out of the evil of their hearts. Yet it was also, possible that this would happen to someone who was not making efforts towards it, as we have mentioned. And therefore, those making efforts to [attain true] prophecy needed an established teacher to teach them, as we have written - so, they would be prevented [from such errors] by him. And all of this is until they would reach the level of true prophecy. For once they reached it, they would already see the great difference and recognize it. Then it would be impossible for them to have doubts about it at all, as we wrote.

Regarding Tsidkiyah the son of Kana'anah and his colleagues: And the matter that happened to Ahab's prophets with the spirit that fooled them is of this type. And that is that on account of his misdeeds, it was decreed about him that he would fall at Ramoth-gilead. So, it was appropriate that there would be a powerful seduction through which he would be drawn and go to that war and not retreat from it, even though that which would happen to him would have appropriately prevent him from it, as actually happened. For Jehoshaphat told him (I Kings 22:5), "Now first seek the word of the Lord," and the prophecy of [Ahab's] prophets did not suffice for him. And all of this was foreseen in front of Him, may He be blessed. And note that when they set up the case in front of the Heavenly court, there were prosecutors and those arguing innocence; but they sought to find ways to fool him. And it came out that the most proper way was through [a certain] spirit. And that is because all of the false prophets had prophesied in front of Ahab, and before his eyes. That means that they were doing those actions to make efforts in such ways as to bring down prophetic revelations. However, they were [really] only making efforts to bring down a revelation of impurity that we mentioned above, and nothing more. [Hence] they were deceiving the king and acting as if they were bringing down [God's] light, may He be blessed. Nevertheless, they were still making efforts to bring it down in front of him. And the revelation that they were actually seeking came down. And this was done before the eyes of the king to strengthen his faith in them more. And this is what is stated in the verse (I Kings 22:10), "and all the prophets were prophesying [in front of them]." And behold what came down to them with that impure prophecy was (I Kings 22:12), "March [...] and triumph, the Lord will deliver it into the king's hand." These were the words that that spirit spoke in their mouths. But they were not mistaken about themselves, as they knew [the nature] of their own efforts. But Ahab was mistaken about them. And he was fooled to the point that he did not believe the words of Michayah, because of his great faith in what he saw from his false prophets. However, Tsidkiyah the son of Kana'anah went further than those prophets. For they only said that which was brought down to them from that spirit, whereas Tsidkiyah went further by doing something like that which was done by the true prophets. And that is because he actually believed in that revelation and thought it to be true and brought down from before [God], may He be blessed, until he went so, far as to wantonly say (I Kings 22:11), "So, said the Lord, 'With these, etc.'" Note that he was not properly learned in the ways of true prophecy, so, he did not distinguish between falsehood and truth. And therefore they, may their memory be blessed, said that he said that which he did not hear. And they likewise, said (Sanhedrin 89a), "The spirit of Naboth fooled him." They furthermore said, "He should have been exacting, according to what Jehoshaphat had told him - that two prophets will not prophesy in the same style [of expression]." In fact, those [false] prophets really did attain a greater revelation at that time than what they were accustomed to attaining, and in a different way than what they were accustomed - to the point that Tsidkiyah erred; and it appeared to him that his prophecy was true this time, even though their efforts were only towards the side of impurity, as we have written. But this was caused by God, as we have written. And understand [this] well.

On Moshe's Unique Status

The difference between all the [other] prophets and our teacher Moses, peace be upon him: More generally, prophecy is divided into two levels: The first is the level of all the prophets besides our teacher Moses, peace be upon him; and the second is the level of our teacher Moses, peace be upon him. And the Holy One, blessed be He, Himself divided them in this [way] and explained their difference in Scripture, (Numbers 12:6-7) "When a prophet of the Lord arises among you, I make Myself known to him in a vision, etc. Not so, with My servant Moses, etc."

The prophecy of the prophets is through a vision or a dream: The prophecy of the category of all prophets besides Moses is through a vision or dream, as it is stated, "I make Myself known to him in a vision, I speak with him in a dream." And that means that the Holy One, blessed be He, makes use of dreaming, which is already embedded in people's nature, to be a means through which to bring down prophecy to the prophet. And it is not that dreaming and prophecy are of the same kind, but rather that dreams are a fitting thing in front of His Wisdom, may He be blessed, through which to bring down prophecy. And they, may their memory be blessed, only said (Berakhot 57b), "A dream is one sixtieth of prophecy," from the aspect of it conveying greater disclosure and information than the regular information that comes to people according to their [conscious] ways of understanding, as we have mentioned above.

And behold that when the flow of prophecy comes upon the prophet, he departs from his perceptions and his senses and is shut down as in sleep; and his thought becomes like the thought of one sleeping and dreaming. And it is then that prophecy is brought down upon him. Regardless, it is possible that this thing reaches a prophet at the time he is awake in the way that we mentioned. But it is [also] possible that the prophecy will be brought down to him when he is laying on his bed through a dream at night. In any event, However, the prophecy will only come to him after he is outside of his senses and shut down in such a trance. Yet it is possible for the thing to happen in very little time, and that he immediately returns to his prior state. Still, at the time of his prophesying, he had left his perceptions and had shut down into a temporary trance until he received the prophecy.

However, the sight of the prophets is only like one who sees though a lens by which one sees images of objects; but they do not see like one who sees his fellow in front of him. Nor do they see like one who sees through one lens, but rather like one who sees through many lenses that project the image one from the other. However, that which is seen is certainly the one [object] - and its movements are [likewise, accurately] seen through the lenses - even if they do not look at it straight on. And not only that, but their vision is only like one who sees though an unpolished lens, such that the object is not completely clear. So, too is it impossible for them to clearly see [God's] glory - even as it is after all the projections of [Its] images - even though what they do truly see is His glory, may He be blessed; and they have no doubt about it at all. And there are also, many levels in this, as well as differences between one prophet and another. For the lens of one may be more polished than that of his fellow and [so, he would be able to] grasp [prophecy] with greater clarity. However, [any] prophet that grasps all this will grasp the matter in truth - meaning it is surely clear to him that what is being revealed and made known to him is from the Creator, may He be blessed; and he grasps the matter of the lens, its existence and its secret. And he perceives, and truly and clearly understands, the understandings with which he is influenced, as we have written above in Chapter 3 (On the Prophetic Experience 1). And yet just as the [divine] glory [that comes] to him is made known through all the projections of the image, so, too is the knowledge that comes to him through riddles and metaphors and through a dream - which is the means through which prophecy arrives, as we have already discussed.

The prophecy of Moses: But Moses' prophecy was superior to all this. And that is, first, that he did not need to depart from his senses and his perceptions, nor to dream at all. Rather prophecy came to him while he was in his regular state. And that is that which is stated about him (Numbers

12:8), "Mouth to mouth will I speak to him." And the matter would be revealed to him like one who sees though a single lens alone, and it itself is polished. And the knowledge would come to him clearly and not through riddles; and that is that which is stated, "and plainly and without riddles." Yet even to him, [God's] glory only appeared according to that which he was able to receive. And it was like the image that is created in a mirror. For in any event, it is impossible for a man to see his Creator. However, it was in such a way that he could at least grasp that image fully and clearly, like one who sees through a polished and bright lens that does not hinder one from seeing. And about this is it stated, "and he observes a picture of the Lord" - for he was able to observe that image that was formed very well. This was not the case for other prophets, as they were not able to master even that image well. And behold that from the image that he was able to grasp, he would attain a great and very clear understanding - more than all the other prophets, as we have written.

And another difference between the other prophets and Moses is that in was not in the hands of the other prophets to prophesy at any time. Rather, they would [only] prophesy at the time that the Creator, blessed be He, wanted to have His prophetic flow rest upon them. But [in the case of] Moses, the matter depended on his own will. And it was given over to his hands to connect with Him, may He be blessed, and to bring down revelation to himself whenever it was needed. Also, the other prophets only received specific matters that the Master, blessed be He, wanted to reveal to them; whereas Moses merited that all the orders of creation be revealed to him. And permission was given to him to examine and to search everything; and all of the keys that were ever given to any people, were given to him. And this is what is stated by the verse (Numbers 12:7), "he is trusted in all My house." And it is likewise, stated (Exodus 33:19), "I will make all My goodness pass before you."

The prophecy of [all of] Israel at the giving of the Torah: Behold just as all of the prophets grasped the image of [God's] glory that was formed for them, as we mentioned, and grasped the secret of the image and its content - meaning, the secret of the existence of this matter that the glory be illustrated, and how this would be brought down and what the intention was of all this - and would grasp secrets of His greatness, may He be blessed, through this image; so, too would they grasp the truth of the thing that He, may He be blessed, has no image at all and that this image was only made for the eyes of the prophet according to His will, may He be blessed, for the reason that is known to Him. And it was stated to Israel about this thing (Deuteronomy 4:12), "And you did not see a picture, but rather a voice"; and likewise, (Deuteronomy 4:15), "for you did not see any picture." As behold that they truly grasped two things: They first grasped that there is no image at all whatsoever to His existence, may He be blessed, and that He is completely devoid of any likenesses. And after this information, a certain prophetic picture was also, revealed to them, about which it was stated (Exodus 24:10), "And they saw the God of Israel, etc." And the Sages, may their memory be blessed, called this (Sifrei Bamidbar 103), a vision of speech. For it does not truly show [God's] glory, but is rather a vision that is formed by the power of speech - which is like the image that is formed with the lens that we mentioned before. For through it, we may grasp specific matters about the secrets of His divinity, may He be blessed, His creation and His direction [of the world], as we have explained.

Derech   Part Three   **Hashem**

Part Four

On Divine Service

Parts of the service [of God]: The whole of the service is divided into two parts: The first is study and the second is action.

Parts of action: Action is divided into four [parts]: The first is constant; the second is daily; the third is periodic; and the fourth is conditional.

The constant is that about which a man is constantly obligated, such as love of God and fear of Him. The daily is that about which he is obligated every day - that is the sacrifices at the time of the Temple; and the prayers and the recitation of Shema now. The periodic is that about which we are obligated at given times, such as Shabbat and holidays. The conditional is that about which we are obligated according to that which comes to us from [life] events, such as the challah -tithe, [other] tithes, redeeming the first born and that which is similar. And in each one of these [categories] is found commands and prohibitions - meaning positive and negative commandments. And they are [the embodiment of] "Veer from evil and do good" (Psalms 34:15).

The essence of the service more generally: In truth, the more general essence of all of these matters was explained in Part I, Chapter 4 (On Human Responsibility 6) - that it is turning to Him, may He be blessed, and seeking His closeness, according to the ways He embedded for us to bring ourselves close, and to cleave, to Him. And see that one must make efforts to remove the barriers of evil clinging to the darkness of physicality and this world, and to strive to come close to Him until we cleave to Him and become perfected through His perfection. For this is His whole desire, may He be blessed, and all of the purpose of His creating the creation, as we have written (Part I, On Human Responsibility 4).

However, the details of these matters are according to the axioms embedded into mankind and into the world in all of their characteristics; and the ways given to man to perfect himself and to perfect all of the creation along with him - according to its arrangements in all of its divisions, roots and branches. And we will now explain some of those that are most relevant and practiced in every place and at all times.

On Torah Study

Behold that Torah study is an obligatory matter. As without it, it is impossible to arrive at [proper] action. For if one does not know what he is commanded to do, how will he do it? However, besides all this, there is in study a great function towards the perfection of man. And we already mentioned the matter briefly in Part I, Chapter 4. Yet now we will write about it at greater length.

Among the influences that are brought from Him, may He be blessed, for the needs of His creatures, it is the most precious and sublime of all that can be found in existence. That means that it is the goal of all that it is the greatest entity of that which can be found that is similar to His true existence, may He be blessed, and the preciousness and sublimity similar to His true sublimity, may He be blessed. And it is that which the Master, blessed be His name, of His glory and preciousness, shares with his servants. However,, the Creator, may His name be blessed, bound this influence to something that which was created by Him, may He be blessed, for this purpose. And that is the Torah. And this matter is accomplished in two ways – by reading and by understanding.

And behold it is obvious that the greater the understanding, the greater the level of influence that will be brought down through it. And one who only understands the wording of the verses cannot be compared to one understands their intent, nor one who understands their surface intent with one who deepens [his understanding] more, nor one who deepens it a little to one who deepens it much. Still, it was from His kindness, may He be blessed, that a level of the influence be brought down with every type of understanding, such that any one who understands [some of] it benefits from the great influence that is bound to that understanding. And even the one who has not reached any understanding, but just speaks [its words], will have it as a means though which some of this influence will also, be meted out to him.

Regarding the parts of the Torah: However, besides this gradation regarding the granting of reward for people's efforts according to the proper measure, there is another differentiation and division according to what requires refinement in the whole of creation. [This is the case] to the point that there is no part of it that is not refined by [Torah study]; such that a part of the creation will [always] be perfected by it. So, it comes out that someone who wants to serve in front of his Creator with complete service must occupy himself with all of its parts according to his ability, so, that the refinement come from him to all parts of the creation. And in this light, they, may their memory be blessed, said (Kiddushin 30a), "A man should always divide his days into three: A third for Scripture; a third for Mishnah; and a third for Gemara." And included in this are all parts of the Torah - such that one divides his time until he has reached all of them. Nor should he relinquish any of them; However, the measure [of time] of his occupation in each of them is fitting to measure according to who he is and according to the events that happen to him. And we have already spoken about this in a separate essay, see there.

Conditions of the study: Now the necessary conditions to accompany the study are these: Awe during the study itself; and constant refinement of [one's] actions. And that is because the whole power of the Torah is only from that which He, may His name be blessed, bound His precious influence to it, to the point that speaking it and understanding it brings down this great influence. But without that, speaking it would not be different from speaking about other affairs or books of wisdom and learning about all the other understandings of natural existence in all its forms. For they only contain knowledge of that matter; but no precious power or elevation comes from it to the spirit of the one that reads, speaks or understands it at all; nor is there any refinement of creation at all. However, the content of this influence is surely divine, as we have written. Moreover, it is the highest and most sublime of the matters that are brought down and come to the creatures from Him, may He be blessed. And since this is so, a man should certainly be in awe and tremble during such an occupation. For it comes out that he is coming forth before his God and occupying himself with the bringing down of the great light from Him towards himself. So, he should surely be embarrassed by his mortal lowliness, and shake from His loftiness, may He be blessed. And he should surely rejoice greatly in his goodly portion that he has merited this - yet with trembling, as we have mentioned. And included in this is that he should not sit with light-headedness nor act with any manner of disrespect - neither towards its words nor towards its books. And if he does this, his study will be what it is truly fitting for it to be, he will bring down that influence that we mentioned, he will gather divine strength to himself and will bring down refinement and emanation for all of the creation. But if this condition is lacking in him, the emanation will not be brought down by him. And his words will be like all human words, his speaking will be like one reading a letter and his thoughts will be like someone thinking about matters of the world. Just the opposite, it will be considered blameworthy for him. For he approached the holy without awe and was light-headed in front of his Creator, while he was still speaking in front of Him and occupied with His holiness, may He be blessed. Hence, according to the level of his awe and the measure of his honor and his carefulness with it, will be the measure of the preciousness of the study and the level of the influence brought down through him, as we discussed earlier.

And the second condition is refinement of [one's] actions. For it is fitting for one who wants to bring down influence to be worthy and readied for the bringing down. Hence if he sullies himself with guiltiness and sins, distances himself from his Creator and is unfaithful to Him [by going] after other powers and evil - it will certainly be said about him (Psalms 50:16), "And to the wicked, God said, 'Who are you to recite My laws, etc.'" And likewise, did they, may their memory be blessed, say, "Anyone who teaches Torah to an unworthy student is like one who throws a stone to Markulis (an idol)." And it is certain that the Torah of such a man will not bring down the influence that we mentioned on any level at all. And nevertheless, the Sages, may their memory be blessed, revealed a great mystery to us: If the evildoers would not abandon Torah study, in the end they would return to the good. For even if they do not have it in their power to bring down anything from in front of Him, may He be blessed - as we have written - [nevertheless,] the words of the Torah are already sanctified on their own. So, they stand on their own, such that from continual occupation with them - one time after another - there will eventually be some arousal and the semblance of the tiniest emanation to the one who is occupied with them. And this is what they, may their memory be blessed, said (Eichah Rabbah, Petichta 2), "If only they had left Me and kept My Torah; for the light in it brings them back to the good." However, it is obvious that these words do not apply to one who is occupied with it in a manner of frivolity and joking or to reveal understandings against the law (halakha). Rather he must at least be occupied with it like one who is occupied with other wisdoms.

The difference in the studies is according to preparation: However, the study of one who purifies and sanctifies himself with his actions draws down influence commensurate to the measure that he prepares himself. So, according to the measure that he increases preparedness, so, does the preciousness of his study and its power increase. That is what we see with the earlier Sages. For the Torah would crown them with a great power and give them stature and preciousness that was not found in the later generations. [This was] because of their greater preparedness than the later ones. And they even said about Jonathan the son of Uziel (Sukkah 28a) that at the time that he was occupied with the Torah, any bird that would fly above him would be burned as a result of the power of the concentration of the Divine Presence that descended upon him through his study.

On Love and Fear of God

Behold, we have already clarified in the first part, fourth chapter, concepts of love and awe/fear, that these are what draw one close and cause one to cleave to one's Blessed Creator. This is said about true love and awe/fear, that is, love of the Blessed Name and not the love of reward, and awe of His greatness, and not fear of punishment. And behold this awe/fear purifies the person from darkness of the physical body, and causes the presence of the Divine Shechina to rest upon one; and in accordance with the amount of awe/fear, so, is the amount of the taharah/purity and the envelopment [of the Divine Shechina], and one who achieves this awe/fear on a constant basis will [merit] the envelopment consistently. And this phenomenon was found with perfection in Moshe/Moses our teacher, peace be upon him. About him is was stated, "Awe/fear for Moshe/Moses was a small matter" (Brachot 32), and so, he merited constant Divine envelopment. It is very difficult for people to achieve true awe/fear as is appropriate, but in accordance with their accomplishment, so, is the power of taharah/purity and holiness for them, as we mentioned, especially while engaged in a mitzvah or in learning. It is [in fact] the necessary condition for completing the learning or the mitzvah, as we mentioned.

On Love: And love is that which makes a man cleave to - and connect with - his Creator, strengthens his power and crowns him with great crowns. And [its] main part is the joy of the heart and the burning of the soul in front of his Creator; and a man's giving himself over with all of his power to sanctify His name, may He be blessed, and to give pleasure in front of Him. And these matters have already been explained in their place and there is no need to write about them at length. And note that connected to this part [of divine service] is faith in Him and His unity, trust, and all similar matters - that make a man cleave to the Creator, may He be blessed, and strengthen him in holiness and emanation.

On the Sh'ma and Its Blessings

Two [acts of] daily worship was imposed upon us, in order to worship in front of Him, may He be blessed. And they are the recitation of Shema and prayer; and at the time of the Temple, [also] the daily and additional sacrifices. And now we will explain their content: Regarding the Unity of His existence, may He be blessed, and the Unity of His control: Behold the first is the recitation of Shema - and its content is His unification and the acceptance of the yoke of His Kingship. And the matter is that the Creator, may His name be blessed, brought all the different entities into existence - the higher and the lower, the spiritual and the physical - and placed them in different arrangements and put into the properties of each of them to act and do deeds, to move in patterns and to move many other things in various ways, according to what His Wisdom, may be blessed, distributed to each and every one. Nevertheless, note that He, may His name be blessed, is the only Root and Cause for all of them. And this matter is understood from two angles - from the angle of existence and from the angle of action. Regarding the angle of existence, we have already explained in Part I (On the Creator 6) how all entities are all dependent upon Him, may He be blessed, and extend from His Will; whereas His existence is a necessary existence from Himself, and is not dependent on anything else besides Him. But all other entities only exist from the angle that He, may His name be blessed, wants them and sustains them with His will. Regarding the angle of action, even though He gave into the properties of the creatures to have control over certain things, according to the scope of their capabilities, and to preform great acts - every one according to its properties - in truth, they surely have no power and control besides that which the Creator, may He be blessed, gave to them. For He is the true Master, Controller and omnipotent One. And all that they do is only that which He, may His name be blessed, gave and gives power to them in order that they should act. But He is the Master over them, to add or take away as He wishes at any minute and at any time. And the depth of the matter is that truly according to the arrangements ordered by His Wisdom, may He be blessed, for the refinement of His creatures - as we wrote in Part I (On the Spiritual Realm 8) - see that there are many matters of evil that move in patterns and move other things in the world; whether from the angle of the free choice of people that sin, or whether from that which is decreed about them to punish them. And at first glance, the matter appears as if it is surely the opposite of His will, may He be blessed. For He, may His name be blessed, surely only wants the good; and all of His desire is to do good. And His name is [even] profaned by the domination of evildoers and the increase of evil things and breakdowns. However, one who knows His ways, may He be blessed and has a deeper understanding of [these] things, knows that all of this nevertheless only causes that - in a deep way - everything brings about the perfection of the creation and will then end with it, as I wrote in Part I (On Mankind 4). So, it comes out that the Holy One, blessed be He, is the One that truly directs everything. And it is only His counsel that stands, such that it will bring His good and His perfection to His creatures, as we wrote there. However, according to the truth of the matter, the things must move in these processes according to the foundations of the amazing Wisdom and the true good. And in the end of all the processes, it will be made known that He, may His name be blessed, is one, a Unity, unique and that He caused all of these causes - in their [various] ways - to come to the true goal, which is the true good that we mentioned. And that which is included in the depth of this thing is the matter of the revelation of the truth of His Unity, may He be blessed. And that is because we have already explained that the aggregate of all the causes in the world are such that, behold, the Creator, may He be blessed, created evil in order for people to remove it and to establish good in themselves and in the creation. And note that there are many axioms and great roots that were planted in this matter, so, that it will be perfected in all of its parts and aspects. For there are truly many details that will be found about the existence of evil in the creation, its actions and its control. And many details will likewise, be found regarding the matter of man's relating to it, and that he is put beneath it and placed among it and in the matter of his overpowering it, opening up his prison and conquering it; and the existence of good and its spreading and its becoming strengthened according to the submission of evil and its being conquered. However, the root of the existence of all evil, its actions and its control are the Creator's hiding His Unity, may He be blessed, such that He not reveal His truth in the world to all. And according to the measure of the hiding is the measure of the power of evil, as we wrote in Part I (On the Spiritual Realm 8). And the root of all the nullification and its removal and the establishment of all the creation with good is the revelation of the truth of His Unity, may He be blessed. And that is what the verse states (Deuteronomy 32:39), "See, then, that I, I am He, etc." and it is [also] written (Isaiah 43:10), "in order that you will know and you will have faith in Me and you will understand that I am He; before Me no god was formed, and after Me, none will be, etc." So, it comes out that the end of the refinement of all the creation is dependent upon the revelation of His Unity, may He be blessed. But surely, He was, is and always will be one, a Unity and unique. However, now He is not revealed to all as is appropriate. But in the future to come, He will be completely revealed to all the creatures, as it is written (Zechariah 14:9), "on that day, He will be one and His name will be one." Yet the Israelites who merited to [receive] His true Torah know this truth and testify to it also, now. And this is that which is written (Isaiah 43:12), "'and you are My witnesses,' says the Lord." And this is a great merit for us. And note that the general direction of this world is divided into the direction of the day and the direction of the night, as we wrote in Part 3, Chapter 1 (On the Soul and its Activities 6). And every morning and every evening, the arrangements and watches of the angels for their assignments are renewed according to the arrangement of [God's] direction. And [accordingly] we - the Children of Israel - are obligated to testify about the truth of His Unity, may He be blessed, from all of the angles. This means whether from the angle of His existence, that He alone necessarily exists, and all of the other entities exist from Him and are dependent upon Him; or whether from the angle of control, that He alone, may His name be blessed, is the unique Controller, and there is no action that is done without the power and authority that He gives to it; whether from the angle of direction, meaning that although there are many great and deep actors, there is no Source besides the One, and there is no Determinant besides the One. This means that He, may His name be blessed, is the cause of everything [coming] to its perfect true purpose. And even though this is not truly revealed now, this is the truth of the matter; and it will be revealed and known at the end of everything.

Regarding His Kingship: And among what still needs to be discerned is that the Creator, may His name be blessed, is surely the King over all of His creatures. And the explanation of this matter is that it is true that His actual existence, may He be blessed, is something that is not dependent on anything besides Him at all and not relative to anything besides Him. For He is surely a necessary and perfect entity on His own. So, He has no relationship with another at all - not above Him and not below Him. This means that He has no cause upon which He is dependent at all - not like something caused with its cause, nor like a component with its complement. And from this aspect, He is called God, blessed be He - meaning the Entity Necessary from Himself, as we have written. However, since He wanted, and created, creatures; and they are all dependent upon Him for their existence, and from all angles, as we have written - from this aspect, He is called the Master of all. For everything is from Him, everything is His; and He controls everything according to His will. Yet in His goodness and His kindness and from His humility, He also, wanted to - as it were - lower His lofty glory to relate to His creatures, even though they do not have a relation to Him at all. And He wanted to be on the level of a king to his people to them; that He be considered like the head and leader and be honored by them - as it were - like a king is honored by his people. [This is] like the matter that is stated (Proverbs 14:28), "With many people is the glory of a king." And from this aspect, we call Him the King of the world. And from this angle, He is certainly considered the Head for us and is honored by us. And we are also, obligated to serve

Him and to obey Him in all that He commands - like a king with his people. So, also, from this aspect are we truly obligated to serve Him and to subjugate ourselves to Him and His decrees, like servants to their king. And this is called accepting the yoke of the Kingship of Heaven, and this matter is included in this verse of Shema Yisrael (Deuteronomy 6:4). That is acknowledgment of this thing, that He is the King of kings of kings, ruling over all of His creatures - the higher ones and the lower ones - and to accept the yoke of His Kingship and be subjugated to Him.

The origin of the testimony over His Unity, and the acceptance of His Kingship: And in truth, great effects for the refinement of the whole creation emanate from these matters. And that is because the arrangements of the creation and its bases are arranged in such a way that when His Kingship, may His name be blessed, is known and all of His creatures acknowledge Him - all good and all tranquility exists for His creatures, blessing is enhanced for them and their welfare grows. But when the servants break loose and do not subjugate themselves and acknowledge His Kingship, may He be blessed, all good is lacking, darkness dominates and evil is in control. And note that these matters in the ways of God are brought down into all parts of creation - the higher and the lower; those that act and those that are acted upon - as we wrote in Part I (On Human Responsibility 7). However, His Kingship being known or not known is certainly drawn down from the actions of the lower beings. And all of these principles have already been explained in their place.

However, that which is important for our matter now is that if there is a reason for the Creator, may He be blessed, to show Himself in His Kingship and rule over His world, much good and great tranquility will come down from this to the creations. And an emanation of holiness, purity and [all] good things grow; whereas the forces of evil will be suppressed and subjugated and will not ruin the good of the world. But if not, the Holy One, blessed be He, hides His face and does not reveal the power of His governance; so, the forces of evil break loose and take control. And all of the effects of this matter are in every place in which it is relevant. And this is the total of all the evil that exists in the world. But surely when Israel strengthens this matter every day and accepts His Kingship, may He be blessed, and acknowledges Him in their hearts and with their mouths, the Holy One, blessed be He, appears in His world and the forces of evil are suppressed by His good; and blessing comes down to the world. And when they testify to His Unity, may He be blessed - as we wrote - corresponding to this does He respond to us and raise Himself up in His Unity and is hence strengthened, to add one refinement to the world after another. [This is] from the aspect of the true refinement that we mentioned, towards which all causes in [God's] direction is [ultimately] leading. He will then fulfill His counsel, which is to place the world in perfect good, as we have written. And from that which you must understand here is that all of these things are only said, such that the refinement of creation will only be from people, and not on its own. For even though the direction is already arranged and fixed in this way, that all of its processes move towards perfection and this is what the Master, blessed be He, caused with His kindness and power - nevertheless His Wisdom decreed that this be done by people. For then people will become perfected when they do this thing, and the perfection itself will be the highest - since the creatures will be the masters of their own perfection. And it comes out that this is the essence of all these things the Master, blessed be He, arranged and prepared to perfect His creation - that they would be perfected and put into effect by people, so, that they be perfected with the perfection that is appropriate for them.

And behold we have already explained in Part I (On the Purpose of Creation 1) that true perfection of creation is in bringing down His perfection, may He be blessed, to it; for He alone has perfection. However, this too is an effect of this commandment. For when we testify to His unity and we condition everything upon Him, He, may His name be blessed, also, becomes available to us; and He is present for all of the creation to perfect itself with His perfection. So, all of the entities will be refined with the true root existence, which is His existence, may He be blessed, as we have written there.

Regarding giving oneself over for the sanctification of His name: And note that that it is one of the conditions of this commandment that a man decide in his mind to give over his life for His Unity, may He be blessed; and to accept all afflictions and types of death for the sanctification of His Name, may He be blessed. And this is considered as if he actually had done it in practice and was killed for the sanctification of His name. And there are also, great effects from this matter for the purpose of the creation and the general refinement. And this is from the arrangements of the Supreme Wisdom about the creatures and their existence that they all be at a given level determined by the Supreme Wisdom to be appropriate for what is desired in this world and its state. And the principle of this level is that it is a level that leaves room for darkness to exist, and for impurity to spread and to act. However, all of this is at a given measure - meaning that there should not exist enough darkness, such that impurity be in control to the point that it makes the world completely impure and corrupts the creatures. For if the [situation] would reach this, they would all need to be destroyed and erased - like what happened at the time of the flood. Rather it should be that some things remain profane and not holy; dark and not bright. And behold that He arranged that this would be their first and basic level. However, by way of a supplement, you will also, find lofty emanations and precious influences from which they can rise from this low level, such that matters of holiness and brightness will reach the creatures according to [the limits] of this world. And see that the things are determined with amazing wisdom - everything appropriately demarcated - not more and not less. And that is that what is appropriate for them as the basic [amount] was determined, and also, divided into specific differing parts and levels; as well as what is appropriate for them by way of a supplement, and that too is divided into specific differing parts and levels. And also, determined were the times that would be appropriate for them to have this supplement according to its levels, as we will write more further with God's help. See that each and every day, an influence and emanation in the creatures needs to occur in order to raise them from the lower level rooted in them and give them holiness and brightness, as we have written. However, the Supreme Wisdom arranged the existence of this invigorating emanation that removes the darkness of the world and increases the preciousness, stature and holiness in it and in its creatures that we mentioned, and made its coming down depend upon the actions of the lower beings - like all the other influences and refinements. In fact, the action that He made it depend upon is a man's giving over his life for the sanctification of His name, may He be blessed. And there are [different] levels in this as well. For when a man gives himself over for the sanctification of [His] name in practice, a great and very strong emanation is brought down and a great refinement comes about in the creation; and there is a great expansion of powerful holiness and brightness. And giving [oneself] over in thought - meaning, to make up his mind to give himself over, as we have written - also, brings down an influence of this type, albeit not as powerful. Nevertheless, for that which needs to occur for the daily bringing down - according to the arrangements of the direction - the giving over in thought is sufficient. And that is what is done in this verse [of Shema]. And the effect that comes out is the bringing down of the influence of holiness and brightness in all of creation, so, as to give it a little elevation from the profane and from the darkness in which it is in on its root level.

It comes out that the aggregate matter in the first verse of Shema is testimony and acknowledgement of His Unity - may He be blessed - in all of His aspects; acceptance of His Kingship and endorsement of His rulership over every one of the creatures at all; and making up one's mind to give up [his life] for the sanctification of His name. And the effect of all this is that the Master, blessed be He, strengthens the governance of His Unity over all of the creation; the submission of and subjugation of the forces of evil; the straightening of the good; and the growth of His being - may He be blessed - found in creation, for it to depend upon Him and become perfected with His perfection. And the influence that elevates the creatures is brought down in the measure that is needed; so, that it gives them brightness and holiness according to what is appropriate.

Regarding Blessed be the name of His glorious Kingship forever and ever: Yet another refinement is joined to this great refinement. And that is that which is included in that which we say, "Blessed is the name of His glory forever and ever." And see that this is because we have already explained that the aggregate of all of His influence, may He be blessed, and His emanations are matters that are brought down by different causes. But they are all rooted and dependent on His Unity and His true perfection. Yet behold the creatures act through various processes, according to the aggregation of these influences and their causes. Nonetheless, the end of everything is that they come to true perfection. Still, it is truly the case that the Supreme Wisdom decreed that it will not be brought down, nor will perfection reach the creatures, except through all of theses causes and after all of the processes. But note that since all of the action and the control is from the Unity, everything is dependent upon Him, and it is known that all of the influences are only branches of the Unity and the way of the creatures to reach It. And see that since it is the intent of the first verse to condition everything upon Him, as we have written, all of the influences are conditioned upon [Him], and everything comes back to the matter of true perfection that we mentioned. And behold what comes out of this for the creatures is that He will have His name descend upon them and His holiness cleave to them with a great cleaving, and that He will rule over them and bring them behind Him, and they will all be found to depend on Him and will perfect themselves with His perfection. And this is the state that they will reach at the end of all the processes. And when they are all like this, it comes out that His will, may He be blessed, will be fulfilled and His glory enhanced. And this is the main crown, in that He is crowned by His creatures; and He is - as it were - aggrandized through them. However, this thing only becomes fulfilled now with the spiritual beings. For behold they are pure and holy, and His name, may He be blessed, rests upon them and is connected to them with a great bond, so, they truly follow behind Him at every hour and at every minute and His glory is thereby enhanced through them. But this matter is not fulfilled with the lower beings, because they are not yet perfect; evil is mixed in with them and they have not purified themselves from it. So, His glory - as it were - is not enhanced by them as is appropriate. So, see that according to the refinement that the angels are in, they recite this praise, "Blessed be the name of His glory Kingship forever and ever." However, it is impossible for the lower beings to recite it, since they are not fit for it, such that [His] name does not rest upon them and His glory is not enhanced by them. But our father Jacob, peace be upon him, merited this already at the time of his leaving the world when he was with all of his holy sons around him, as there was no disqualification among them. So, they were crowned by His Unity, may He be blessed, when they said, "Shema Yisrael, etc." And then the elder (Jacob) answered them, "Blessed be the name of His glorious Kingship forever and ever." So, it comes out that we are not worthy of this matter on our own. However, a little of it was given to us because of our father Jacob. So, therefore we only say it in a whisper, except on Yom Kippur. For on [that day], Israel rises up to the level of the angels - as we will discuss in its place with God's help.

The first passage of the recitation of Shema: And truly, the other passages are the completion of this matter. And the matter consists of three principles. And they are the acceptance of the yoke of His Kingship and love for Him; acceptance of the yoke of commandments; and remembering the exodus from Egypt. In the first passage (Deuteronomy 6:4-9), a man should have the intention to strengthen his love for Him, may He be blessed, under all conditions - meaning "with all your heart, with all your life and with all your power." [Likewise,] to bring down the emanation of His holiness, may He be blessed, and His Kingship, may He be blessed, to his children and to all of his progeny - that is, "And you shall teach them to your children." [And likewise, also] to refine oneself in every type of state that a man is in - which is "when you sit in your house and when you walk, etc." And to refine the aspect of his house - and that is "And you shall write, etc."

The remembrance of the exodus from Egypt: Afterwards, he accepts the yoke of commandments upon himself with [the passage that begins with,] "And if you listen" (Deuteronomy 11:13-21). And then he mentions the exodus from Egypt with the passage (Numbers 15:37-41) of the fringes (tsitsit). For the exodus from Egypt was a great refinement in which we - Israel - were refined, and the matter stayed forever. And that is because after the sin of Adam, all of humanity remained corrupted, as we have written in Part I (On Mankind 5). And evil was growing until there was no place for the good to strengthen itself at all. And even though our father Abraham, peace be upon him, had been selected - they still did not have a place where they were able to strengthen themselves and establish themselves as a whole nation and merit the crowns that were fit for them, due to the evil that was darkening them and to the earlier pollution that had not yet left them. And hence it was necessary for them to be exiled to Egypt and be subjugated there; such that in that great subjugation, they were refined like gold in a crucible and were purified. And so, when the appropriate time came, the Master, blessed be He, strengthened His influence and emanation over Israel, suppressed the evil in front of them, separated them from it, elevated them from their lowliness and raised them to Him. So, they were redeemed with a permanent redemption; and from then on, they were established as a whole nation cleaving to Him, may He be blessed, and crowned by Him. And note that this was a refinement that was made forever, as we have mentioned. And all of the good that has come and is coming to us is all dependent upon this. Hence, we have been commanded to always remember it and to mention it with our mouths. For through it, this refinement is strengthened upon us, the light is intensified in us, and the purpose that comes out of this refinement is perpetuated.

The two hundred and forty-eight words: However, there is another refinement included in the recitation of these passages. And that is to refine man in all of his aspects in the light of His Unity - as well as to refine all parts of the creation. This is since the sum of all of the specific aspects of man are truly two hundred and forty-eight, which [corresponds] to his two hundred and forty-eight limbs. Moreover, the parts of creation are also, two hundred and forty-eight - according to their foundations - parallel to the two hundred and forty-eight limbs of a man. And both these and those require refinement from the light of His Unity, may He be blessed. And the refinement is through the two hundred and forty-eight words in the recitation of Shema.

The blessing over the recitation of Shema in the morning: And behold that the Sages, may their memory be blessed, attached the blessing over the recitation of Shema to this. And that is because all of existence is completely renewed before Him, may He be blessed, every day. And this is from two aspects. The first is from the aspect of survival and perpetuation, since He renews the influence over everything for them to survive and perpetuate themselves in their existence. And the second is since all the days of the six thousand years are surely all decreed and prepared in front of Him in the aspect of [their] emanations, influences, realities and necessary states for the world to finish the desired cycle and reach perfection. So, it comes out that each day is a truly new aspect. And from that [particular] aspect, all of existence is completely renewed. And about this is it said [in the blessings], "He renews the act of creation every day." And behold it is upon this foundation that they established these blessings and praises upon the whole of all the creatures - as they are renewing themselves one day after another. And behold the sum of these creatures is divided into two. The first is all of the creatures of the world - the lower ones and the higher ones. And the second is the collective of the human specie. And that is Israel, for they are truly the specie of man. And see that it is upon this arrangement that they arranged the first blessing with the praise for all of the creatures and their supervisors - which are the creatures below and the angels above - each one in its arrangements. And they included in this the matter of night and day and the luminaries that rule in them. And the second is in praise of the matters [relating to] Israel, the love with which He loves them and the closeness with which He drew them to His service. And all of these things were included in these blessings in their true ways. Afterwards, [he] recites Shema. And afterwards, they arranged another blessing on the sum of the great miracles that the Master, blessed be He, did for us. And the main one was the exodus from Egypt in its details, organized according to its true secrets and to all of its aspects.

The blessing over the recitation of Shema in the evening: And see that the essence of the matter is in the morning, as the renewal of existence is then - as we have written. Nevertheless, new content is added to the creatures at night, according to the character of the night. But this is only like the end of the content of the day and its completion. And from this angle, they also, arranged the blessing over the recitation of Shema in the evening to be just like the blessings over the recitation of Shema in the morning - only shorter. For it is only a review of the things in short - just like that which renews itself in the arrangements of [God's] direction flows from that which was renewed during the day. And they also, added a blessing over the matter of rest at night, and over sleep in all of its aspects - and that is the blessing [that begins], "Lay us down."

On Prayer

Regarding prayer: The matter of prayer is surely from the arrangements that were set up by the Supreme Wisdom for this reason: Since the creatures receive bounty from Him, may He be blessed, there is a need for them to arouse themselves towards Him and seek His presence. So, the bounty comes down to them according to the arousal towards Him. But if they do not arouse themselves, it does not come down to them. And behold the Master, blessed be He, desires and wants that the good of His creatures be increased at all times; so, He prepared this worship for them on a daily basis. For through it, bounty, success and blessing will come down to them according to their needs [and] according to their situation in this world.

However, there is greater depth to the matter. And that is that the Master, blessed be He, surely gave man the intellect to manage himself in this world with his intelligence and his understanding. So, He placed the task upon him to oversee all of his [own] needs. And this matter is based on two foundations: The first one is that because of man's preciousness and importance, he was given this intelligence and intellect to administer himself properly. The second is that he should have an occupation in the world and be bound to his affairs. And this is what sustains him in the human condition, which we mentioned above - such that it is the worldly approach and not the holy approach. But it is what he needs at this time, according to the arrangements of [God's] direction. Of course, from one angle, this diminishes him and his status. But it is a necessary diminution for him, that brings about an elevation for him afterwards, as was explained in Part I (On Human Responsibility 4). However, even as this diminution is necessary according to his situation in this world; from another angle, he needs not to go beyond what is appropriate. For note that the more he gets embroiled in the matters of the world, the more he will distance himself from the Supreme light and become more darkened. But see that the Creator, may He be blessed, prepared a rectification for this. And that is that a man first come close, stand in front of Him, may He be blessed, request all of his needs and 'cast his burden upon' Him. And this is a central and essential beginning for all of his efforts, such that when he is later pulled into the other ways of effort - which are the ways of human effort - it will not happen that he will get embroiled and stuck in physicality and materialism. For he will already have begun with, and made everything dependent upon, Him, may He be blessed. So, his diminution will not be a major diminution, but will rather be held up by this rectification that comes before it.

The matter of approaching prayer and the three steps after it: And behold that it was from His kindness, may He be blessed to give man a space in which to come close to Him, may He be blessed - even though according to his natural state, he is found to be far from the light and stuck in the darkness. And that is that He gave him permission to stand in front of Him and call out in His name. And then he rises from the lowliness - which is his temporary condition - and finds himself close in front of Him and 'casts his burden upon' Him, as we have written. And behold this is [the reason for] the stringency of prayer, according to which it is forbidden to interrupt it at all - due to man's being in great proximity to Him, may He be blessed. And likewise, is the leave-taking set up at its end, such that a man takes three steps back and returns to his regular state, which is needed by him the rest of the time.

And in truth, [the Sages], may their memory be blessed, informed us of the necessary conditions accompanying prayer in order to fulfill its function - whether regarding this coming close that we mentioned, or whether regarding the bringing down of the influence. And they set up prayer and its blessings for us accordingly, and prescribed all of its laws and guidelines.

But behold that which we explained until now about the recitation of Shema and about prayer is only according to the function of these commandments in terms of what they are [in themselves]. However, they additionally set up an arrangement of prayer for us that is also, fit to substitute for the sacrifices now missing. And that is what is necessary with the arrival of every day according to the axioms of time in all of its parts. But this will be explained below in the next chapter with God's help.

On the Daily Order of Prayer

Regarding the control of the forces of impurity at night: The Supreme Wisdom set up that at night, the forces of impurity be given the authority to spread through all of its channels, and for its branches to wander throughout the world. And He intended that at that time, people would gather into their houses, lay down in their beds, sleep and rest until the morning. For [in the morning] the spreading and authority of these forces and all of their branches would be taken away; and people would once again leave to 'their work, until the evening.' And this is what King David, peace be upon him, explained (Psalms 104:20-23), "You bring on darkness and it is night, etc. When the sun shines, etc. Man goes out to his work, etc." However, all of these matters - in all of their demarcations and measures - are rooted in the roots of the foundations of [God's] direction, according to all of its influences that come to the creatures at all of their levels, as it is written in Part I (On the Spiritual Realm 3), see there. But you should know that even though it is said by way of generalization, that the night is the time that these forces are given authority, note that it is actually only given during the first half of the night. But from midnight, an influence of emanation and will flows from in front of Him, may He be blessed, to all of the worlds. And authority is [then] taken from the forces of evil; and their branches are driven away from the place of civilization. So, the emanation of the day begins to be aroused until the day is brightened by [the sun's rise]. And then the proper influence is brought down and all of existence is renewed. However, the matter of this authority of these forces at night and their being driven away is a thing that is embedded into the nature of the world and its arrangements. [It is] beyond the authority and submission that comes to them from the actions of man. And that is that the Supreme Wisdom determined that since the existence of true good and evil is something that follows from the actions of the ones with free choice, it was necessary that there be an avenue within the natural axioms of the world for evil to have authority in it in such a way that it would be possible for this evil to spread in parts of it, as well as its being prevented from spreading [in other parts of it]. And truly since this is so, the Supreme Wisdom decreed that it be appropriate that there be one part in time itself, in which He would give it authority and [the possibility] to spread on its own. And see that it is the schema upon which it is possible to add from the actions of man. And [It likewise, decreed] that there be another part in which authority would be taken away from it, such that there be a basis in which it be possible for [man's] actions to be the [sole] cause. And behold that the two powerful entities of light and darkness follow from the angle of [God's] emanation and its absence, as we explained in Part I (On the Purpose of Creation 3); and He gave them [each] a portion in time, meaning day and night. And the authority of the powers of impurity - that we mentioned - and their being driven out follow [these times]. But it is all [only] the substructure for the effects of the actions [of man], as we have mentioned.

Regarding the impurity of the hands at night: Moreover, when this authority is given to these powers of evil, and in their spreading in the world, it comes out that the darkness of the world increases and is strengthened. And the spreading of impurity that wanders in the world also, spreads in man - even as he is laying in his bed - according to the measure that it is able to do so, based on its connection to the body of that man, from the perspective of its physicality and the evil impulse in it. And in addition to this, it was already prepared in the ways of [God's] direction that when man sleeps, parts of his higher soul retreat, as we wrote in Part II (Part III, On the Soul and Its Activities 6), and [so] he tastes a little of the taste of death. And this is that which they, may their memory be blessed wrote (Berakhot 57b), "Sleep is one sixtieth of death." And it comes out that darkness overpowers his darkened body more when the light of the soul is missing and is not purifying it. Hence there is more of an entrance for impurity to rest upon it. And this is the matter of evil spirit (ruach ra'ah) that they, may their memory be blessed, explain rests upon the hands (Shabbat 109b). However, its resting upon the hands and not upon any other place is because this is the measure and limit that the Supreme Wisdom determined to be appropriate that it rest upon a man, according to his state in the world - not less and not more.

And see that the Supreme Wisdom set up for man, that he makes efforts in the morning and elevate himself from being in a degraded state at night; to purify himself from having become impure. He [must] bring the whole world back and elevate it from that which it was degraded and bring light to it from the darkness with which it was darkened. And this matter is completely included in the ordinances - of acts and

Derech — Part Four — Hashem

of words - that were ordained for the time of rising up, as we will write with God's help.

Washing of the hands (netilat yadayim): Behold the first act is the purification of the hands, because they are that which became impure and upon which evil spirit rested; so, one must drive it away from them and purify them. And behold the Creator, may He be blessed, embedded that they be driven away through the appropriate washing, as they, may their memory be blessed, taught us. And it comes out that his whole body is purified by this, just as all of it had been impure from the resting of evil spirit on [the hands]. And there is also, a refinement of the whole entire creation with this matter, to be purified from the impurity of the night and to exit from its darkness. And behold they also, connected a man's cleaning his body after relieving himself to this [action]. And it comes out that he is [then] totally purified and prepared to come close in front of his Creator.

After this, However, come two acts that are even included in the 613 commandments on their own; but they are [also] connected with the practices of prayer, to complete the daily service. And they are fringes (tsitsit) and tefillin. But we will first explain their specific contents; and afterwards, we will explain their levels in the practices of the daily service that we mentioned.

The tsitsit: The content of the tsitsit is that the Master, blessed be He, surely wanted that Israel be refined concerning matters of holiness from every angle. Therefore,

He gave them commandments for all of their times, and according to all of their situations, such that they be refined in all of them. And surely included in what pertains to man are the clothes he wears. So, in order that they too be refined, He commanded that they place the tsitsit upon them. Then they would be refined with holiness. And there is a deeper matter than this also, included in the commandment. And that is that a man be marked for his God, like a slave is for his master. And this is included in the acceptance of His yoke, may He be blessed, and subjugating oneself to His yoke, may He be blessed. And behold it is possible for man to refine the entire creation as explained in Part I (On Human Responsibility 7). So, it comes out that he is occupied with His work, as he brings the creation that He created to the state that He, may He be blessed, desires. And this is truly affected by the acts of man, and the deeds that he does according to the Torah and the commandment [given] to him. However, the main principle of this service stands on one foundation, which is that man be the servant of the Creator, blessed be He. For this matter of refinement has been given over to him; and it is in hands for this matter to be successful, and it is his acts that will bring about these effects. Indeed, since the whole of existence is [balanced] on this task upon man - which is called His yoke, may He be blessed, and is like the yoke of a master upon his slave - this thing is strengthened by given details that the Master, blessed be He, made it depend upon. And among them is being identified and stamped with this stamp of the tsitsit. Moreover, beyond this thing being a constant commandment, the Sages, may their memory be blessed, made it into one of the practices of prayer. And that is that one wraps himself in a shawl (a talit with tsitsit) to pray in it. And the practice is an acceptance of the yoke that we mentioned - as with its power, he grabs and holds His work, may He be blessed, which is the refinement of the world, as we wrote.

Tefillin: However, the content of tefillin is much greater than tsitsit. And that is that the Creator, may He be blessed, granted that Israel truly bring down His holiness, may He be blessed; and that they be crowned by it in such a way that all of their spiritual and physical characteristics be sheltered under this great light; and that they [also] create a great refinement through it. And this is what the verse states (Deuteronomy 28:10), "And all the nations of the world will see that the name of the Lord is called upon you." And this matter is dependent upon this commandment, in all of its laws and details. Moreover, there are two main organs in a person from which the soul derives great strength. And they are the brain and the heart. And the Creator, may He be blessed, commanded that this light first be brought down into the brain through the head tefillin and that the brain, and the soul in it, be refined through it. Then it expands afterwards to the heart through the arm tefillin that is across from it, so, that it too is refined by it. And through this, it comes out that man is completely included in the drawing down of this holiness to all of his characteristics; he is crowned by it and attains a great holiness. Notwithstanding, there are various details found in the conditions of the commandment: Matters are found in all of their parts that are needed for the desired refinement of all of his parts, according to the division of the characteristics of man.

Days upon which there is no tefillin: And behold we were commanded to be crowned with this crown every day except for holy days - which are themselves a sign for Israel. Hence Israel is crowned through them (the holidays) without any other effort - which is not the case on other days. For it is impossible to acquire the crowns [then] without this effort (of tefillin). But even after this personal effort, the crown that is achieved by them is not on the level of the crown achieved automatically on holy days, but rather much less than it. Yet all things are determined according to what is most appropriate, with all of their limits, by the Supreme Wisdom.

And behold once a man is distinguished with tsitsit and crowned with tefillin, the orders of prayer are set up for him, to refine that which is necessary. And the general intention is to uphold all of creation - all of the worlds - in a proper state that is fit to have the supreme bounty flow upon it; and to bring down the flow from in front of Him, may He be blessed, according to what is necessary.

The sections of prayer: However, the whole of prayer is divided into four sections: The first is the sacrifices; the second is the verses of song (pesukei dezimrah); the third is the recitation of Shema and its blessings; and the fourth is [the actual] prayer and that which follows it. The general intention of the sacrifices is to purify all the world, and to remove anything from it which would be an interference or a prevention for the coming of the supreme flow down to it. The general intention of the verses of song is to reveal the light of His presence, may He be blessed, through the praises with which we praise Him and recount His acclaim. For the Creator, may He be blessed, made it depend on this act, meaning praising Him. And this is the [meaning] of "the One who chooses the verses of song" (at the end of this section). We have already explained the general content of the recitation of Shema and its blessings. But besides that, there is another matter. And that is that which we have already explained in Part I (On the Spiritual Realm 3), that the orders of the creation's setup and its unfolding is such that - besides all of the creatures unfolding one level after another from the root forces to the physical ones - the Highest Wisdom set up that since the creatures all receive flow from in front of Him, may He be blessed, they first be connected one to another from the bottom up. [So] the bottom ones [are connected] to the ones above them and the higher ones to the ones above them and so, on, in this way, until the root forces; and they [in turn] depend upon Him, may be blessed - such that He flows upon them [first] and they then spread the flow from above to below through all of the levels of the creation, as is appropriate. They then come back and all stand upon their levels for their tasks, according to that which is arranged for them. Moreover, these blessings over the recitation of Shema are ordered according to these secrets. So, with this acclaim and praise, the levels of creation rise from below to above until they are all bound to the highest level. And then everything is bound and dependent upon His light, may He be blessed; and His flow comes down to all of the creatures, which is that which is done in the prayer of the eighteen (shmoneh esreh) [blessings].

Regarding the eighteen blessings: And behold, you should know that the types of supreme influence - under which all types of flow and their details are included - are three. And they are indicated in the three [first] letters of [His] name, blessed be He; and their binding together for the perfection of all creation is indicated by the last [letter in His name,] hay. And corresponding to them are the three descriptions [in the first blessing], "the Great, the Powerful and the Awesome." And that which brings them down as is fit is the merit of Abraham, Isaac and Jacob; whereas that which brings down the perfection that comes out of their connection is the merit of King David, who connects with the patriarchs and completes the refinement of Israel. And note that the first three blessings of the prayer were ordained to correspond to these three types [of influence]. So, the supreme influence is brought down more generally through them. And afterwards, they are brought down in detail by the intermediate [blessings], according to the need. And through the last three, they are strengthened and internalized by those receiving them, through the thanksgiving which they give to Him. And this is the general refinement of all of prayer.

The seven blessings of Shabbat: But whereas the thing is brought down according to this order on weekdays, the Sages did not burden a man with more than seven blessings on holy days. For see that the day is holy and blessed on its own, and [so] it helps to bring down the flow. Hence it is enough for a person to a make an effort more generally. And that is the seven blessings - the first three concerning the three types [of influence], and likewise, the last three, as we wrote above. And the middle one is about the holiness of the day, such that it should be strengthened, give light and rule; and it is [also] what will help and fulfill all of the details. And we will speak more about this further.

The four worlds: And you also, need to know that the sum of worlds is divided into four. And that is this world in both of its parts - the higher and the lower - which are the heavenly part, which is called the world of the spheres; and the foundational one, which is called the lowly one. But the sum of them both is called one world. And above this world is the world of the angels; and above it is the world of the higher forces - the roots of the creatures that we mentioned in Part I (On the Spiritual Realm 1). And it is called the world of the throne. And behold above this in level, one can distinguish the sum of His influences, may He be blessed, [and] the revelation of His light, though which all of what is in existence comes down and is dependent upon, as we wrote in Part III, Chapter 2 (On Divine Names and Witchcraft 4). But behold it is by way of a borrowed term that the sum of all of these influences is called a world. And it is called the world of divinity. However, you can surely see that this name is only applicable to it as a borrowed term, as we have written - for the reason that we will explain - something that is not the case with the first three worlds. For with them, the word truly fits. And that is because the word, world, is used for a group of many phenomena and varying entities in a place in which they are divided into many parts and in which they relate to each other in various ways. So, note that with phenomena - be they physical or spiritual - this matter is truly possible. Hence this world is called a world since it is a group of lowly and heavenly bodies in one place. And the world of angels is called a world since it it also, a group of many angels in one place, such as [place] applies to them. And the world of the throne is a world since it is a group of many powers in the place that is relevant. However, His influences, may He be blessed, are not many phenomena and various entities at all. Rather they are [abstract] distinctions and types of light from Him, may He be blessed. For their content is only that which He, may His name be blessed, makes available to His creatures and with which He activates them according to their properties. Nevertheless since we can distinguish differences, orders and levels among these influences, according to that which is fit for those that receive them - in which the differences, orders and levels are recorded, as we have written in Part III, Chapter 2 (On Divine Names and Witchcraft 4) - the sum of all this is therefore called a world. But we consider it higher, above all the [other] three. For it is like this according to the gradation. And surely all of the unfolding rises up from this physical level to the angels; and the angels to that which is above them - which is the throne and its levels; and the throne to His influences, may He be blessed, and the revelation of His light - which is the true root of everything.

The correspondence of the sections of prayer to the worlds: And behold that it was according to this order that the divisions of prayer were ordained. Hence the three sections at the beginning are for the refinement of the three worlds - this world, the world of the angels and the world of the throne. And that [corresponds to] the sacrifices, the verses of song and the blessing over the Shema. Afterwards is the standing prayer, which corresponds to the world of divinity, to bring down the influences according to their distinctions. And there are three other parts afterwards to bring down the duration of flow to the worlds - one after another, until the end. And they are the sanctification of the order (kiddushah de'sidrah), the song of [the day of] the Levites and "There is none like our God." And after all this is Aleynu; and it is to return and affirm His Kingship, may He be blessed, over all the worlds, after they were all blessed.

Regarding the [supplication] and the thirteen attributes: And see that a few other specific matters were connected to this to arouse His mercy and to enhance the blessing. And included in this is the matter of the confession, the mention of the thirteen attributes [of mercy] and the falling on the face (the supplication or tachanun). And that is because the confession is to seal the mouths of the accusers, such that they do not cause one's prayer to be pushed off, God forbid.

The power of the mention of the thirteen attributes is that the Master, blessed be, grabs the trait of His mercy and - through the control of His preeminence - passes over transgression and grants grace, even in the absence of merit. And the falling on the face is also, a great submission in front of Him, may He be blessed, which has great power in appeasing the trait of [strict] justice, such that great mercy is aroused and [His] flow is brought down with plenitude and largesse. However, this is the general order upon which prayer is based. Yet there are many details to this outline, upon which the particulars of the order - such as the hymns and the other verses - depend, as each thing was ordained in its place.

Regarding the afternoon (mincha) and evening (arvit) prayers and (tikkun chatsot): And you need to know that within the arrangements for [God's] direction of the day, it is surely divided into two parts: The morning; and after midday, which is the afternoon. And the night is also, divided into two parts, and as we have written above. However, the arousal and influence to the worlds must continue in all of them, according to the characteristic of that time period. And because of this, they arranged the prayers according to their [actual] number. And that is that during the two parts of the day, they ordained the morning prayers and afternoon (mincha) prayers. But behold in the morning, which is the time of the renewal of the flow according to the attribute of day, they ordained the order to be lengthy, according to all that is necessary. But for the second half of the day, which follows from the first, it only requires a little effort in order to complete the matter, corresponding to that period of time. But since there is a greater change with the night - because of the change of the characteristics, meaning the [arrival of the] characteristic of night, which is more different than the change from morning to afternoon - they therefore ordained a longer order [of prayer] than in the afternoon, and that is with the blessings over the Shema. Yet it is shorter than in the morning, since the flow is nevertheless already coming down from the morning. However, for the second part of the night, in order not to burden the community (at such an inconvenient time), they did not fix an order [of prayer] for everyone at all. Rather they left the matter to the pious ones, to get up and chant - each one according to his ability. And even the night prayer service itself was already just optional - and they [only later] set it up as an obligation - all the more so, the rectification of midnight (tikkun chatsot). And behold, see that the patriarchs ordained the three prayer services (Berakhot 26b). And from this angle, it is incumbent upon on all of Israel to follow their order (and say all three). However, it was David that was alacritous with the rectification of the second part of the night, as it is stated (Psalms 119:62), "I arise at midnight to praise You." And he is the one who complements the patriarchs in their refinement of Israel, as we wrote above. However, the matter was not fixed for all of Israel, but rather for their pious ones - since they are on a level slightly below the patriarchs.

The additional (musaf) prayer: And note that on holy days, there is the addition of a prayer corresponding to the additional sacrifice. And it is in the character of the added flow of that day, according to its characteristic holiness and content.

On Divine Service and the Calendar

The periodic service is that about which we have been obligated on specific times. And their specifics are the rest on Shabbat and its holiness; the tenth [of Tishrei] (Yom Kippur) and its afflictions; the rest on the holidays and the holiness of the intermediate days of the festival; chamets and matsah in their time; shofar in its time, sukkah and lulav in their time; and the new month, Chanukah and Purim. And now we shall explain their contents:

Regarding the holy Shabbat: The general content of Shabbat is [as follows]: We have already explained above that the matter of this world is to allow for there to be things that are profane and not holy. However, it was also, necessary from another angle that there also, be some holiness to the creatures, so, that the darkness not overwhelm them more than is necessary. And see that the Supreme Wisdom determined all of this with extreme precision - to which level the profane should reach and to which level this added holiness should reach. And It limited all of this with proper delineations in terms of quantity, quality, place, time and all the [other] characteristics with which one can distinguish entities. In any event, regarding time, it organized the matter of days of the profane and days of the holy; and in the holy days themselves, levels, one above the other, according to what is appropriate. And note that It set up that there be more days of the profane than days of the holy, and that there only be holiness according to the needed measure. However, it decreed that the days all revolve around a measure of one set number, such that all time revolve around it. And that is the number of seven days. This is because all of existence was created in this amount. And all of the present is included in this number; so, it comes out that this number is called the full measure. For all of it is needed for the presence of all existence, but more than it is not needed at all, since all of what exists was completed within it. Yet this number passes and then repeats itself in its cycles until the end of all the six thousand [years]. Moreover, all the days of the entire world also, observe this measure in the larger amount - meaning six thousand [years] and then one thousand years of rest. And afterwards, existence will be renewed in a different arrangement, according to the decree of the Supreme Wisdom. But note that It ordered that the end of the cycle always be with the holy; and this comes out to be an elevation for all of the days. For even though most of them are profane and only one-seventh is holy, it is what is required for this world - as we mentioned. Moreover, from another angle, since this portion is the end of the cycle and its seal, it comes out that what is around it is refined and elevated through it, to the point that all of man's days become sanctified. And behold that this is a great gift that the Holy One, blessed be He, gave to Israel; as He wanted that they be a holy people to Him. But He did not give it to the [other] nations at all, as this level is not fit, nor designed, for them.

Prohibition of work on the holy Shabbat: However, it is proper that on this day, Israel behave according to this level that they arrive upon it. And we have already explained above (Part 1, On Mankind 3) that involvement in the world is what connects a person to physicality, lowers his character and downgrades him from this level and preciousness that was fit for him. And for this reason, he must withdraw [from it] on Shabbat, since his character is elevated from that which it is on weekdays, so, he needs to comport himself worthily according to this level. However, it is impossible to completely withdraw from physicality and from his occupation - as he is nevertheless in this world, and his physical bonds are upon him. But the Supreme Wisdom determined the level of disengagement from physicality that would be appropriate and the level that he must stay on. So, It commanded him to withdraw to the level at which it is fitting for him to withdraw, and warned him not to fail from withdrawing. And this is the general principle of all the work that is prohibited on Shabbat.

Delighting in the Shabbat and honoring it: And besides that, we are forbidden to violate the honor of the holiness that flows on this day - as we have written - we were also, commanded [to] honor this holiness that flows. And that is the principle of the delighting (oneg) in the Shabbat, and honoring (kavod) it upon its entering and leaving, with Kiddush and Havdalah [respectively]. And the rest of all of its details are matters generally based upon this fundamental principal, which is to keep ourselves properly worthy for the holiness that flows upon us [on Shabbat]; and to cherish it, in honor of its content - which is great closeness to Him, may He be blessed, and great cleaving to Him - and to honor that He, may He be blessed, gave us such a big gift as this. And the details of [these] matters correspond to the details of this holiness, its characteristics, its ways and its effects, according to what they actually are.

The other holy days: However, the Supreme Wisdom decreed to add holiness upon holiness to Israel and gave them holy days besides the Shabbat, in which Israel would receive levels of holiness. Yet all of them are below the level of Shabbat, its influence and its holiness. And see that according to the level of the influence of these days is our need to withdraw from worldly occupations; and according to this is the prohibition of work on them: And that is that Yom Kippur is above all of them; after it are the holidays; after them are the intermediate days of the festival; after them is the new month (Rosh Chodesh) on which only women refrain from work; and after all of them are Chanukah and Purim, upon which there is no refraining from work, but rather thanksgiving on Chanukah [and Purim], as well as joy on Purim. And all of this is according to the measure of the flow and the light that are bestowed [on any given day].

Celebration of the periodic holidays: But besides this holiness that was determined about their levels according to the level of the holiness of these days, there are other specific attributes to each time period according to its content. And the root of them all is the order arranged by the Supreme Wisdom, such that the refinement refined and the great light that shone at a particular time return at that period of the year to shine light similar to the first light and have the effect of the refinement be renewed in the one that received it [originally]. So, see that, according to this, we were commanded on the holiday [of Passover] about all the things that we are commanded in memory of the exodus from Egypt. For since that refinement was a very great refinement that happened to us - as we wrote above - it was embedded that upon the return of that period of the year, a light similar to the light that shone then, shine; and that the effect of that refinement be renewed in us. Therefore, we were commanded in all of those matters. And in the same manner, the holiday of Pentecost (Shavuot) for the giving of the Torah; and the holiday of Tabernacles (Sukkot) for the clouds of glory. Even though [the latter] is not specifically at the same time, the Torah fixed this holiday for the memory of that matter, as it is stated (Leviticus 23:43), "that I placed them in huts, etc." And likewise, Chanukah, and likewise, Purim [have observances tied to the events they commemorate). And in this same manner were all the days [listed] in the Scroll of Fasting, but they were annulled since Israel was not able to keep them. So, they were exempted from memorializing them and from the arousal of the [corresponding] shining light. And now we will explain these commandments on their own.

On Seasonal Commandments

Regarding chamets and matsah: The content of chamets (unleavened grain products) and matsah is that until the exodus from Egypt, Israel was subservient to the other nations - a nation inside another. But in their exodus, they were redeemed and separated out. And behold that until that time, all the aspects of people's bodies were darkened by overpowering darkness and pollution. But with the exodus, Israel was separated, and their bodies were prepared to become pure and to be ready for the Torah and for [divine] service. And it was for this function that they were commanded about the destruction of chamets and the eating of matsah. Indeed, this is because the bread that is prepared for human sustenance is truly equal to the desired state of man. As the matter of leavening is that it is a natural thing in bread, in order for it to be easily digestible and have a good taste. Behold this is also, that which follows from the proper nature of man, as he also, needs that the evil impulse and the penchant for the physical (equated with leavening) be in him. Yet for a specific and determined time, Israel needed to refrain from chamets and to be sustained by matsah, so, as to diminish the strength of the evil impulse and the penchant for the physical in themselves, and to enhance their drawing near to spirituality. Yet it would be impossible for them to always be sustained like that, since this is not what is desired in this world. However, it is fit that they should keep this matter during the days designated for it. For through this, they will maintain the level appropriate for them. And behold this is the main content of the Holiday of Matsot (Passover). And the other commandments of the first night are all specific matters parallel to the details of that redemption.

The sukkah and the lulav : The content of the sukkah and the lulav is [as follows]: Behold it is that the clouds of glory with which the Holy One, blessed be He, surrounded Israel had a great spiritual effect - in addition to their physical purpose, which was to cover them and protect them. And it was that just like Israel found itself separated alone, and lifted up from the earth by these clouds; so, too were they brought to an emanation that housed them separately from all the nations, literally uplifted and removed them from the world itself and actually made them superior to all the nations of the world. And this matter occurred at that time to Israel, when they reached the highest-level fit for them. And this effect was passed on to each person in Israel for all generations. For indeed the light of holiness is drawn from in front of Him, may He blessed, and surrounds every righteous person in Israel, separates him from all people, raises him above them and places him higher than all of them - and this is something that is renewed in Israel by the sukkah on the festival of Sukkot. And with the waving of the lulav (palm frond) and its [three associated] species, the light of God, blessed be He, shines upon the heads of Israel and crowns them in such a way that their fear falls upon all of their enemies. And that is what is written (Deuteronomy 28:10), "And all the nations of the world will see that the name of the Lord is called upon you." And they would have even openly attained this matter right away, if sins had not prevented it. However, the thing is nevertheless ready to go into effect in its time. And through the details of the commandment of the lulav - its waving's and its circling's - this matter is fulfilled, to strengthen the control of God, blessed be He, over the heads of Israel and to bring down their enemies in front of them; until they themselves will choose to be their servants. And this is the matter that is stated (Isaiah 49:23), "they shall bow to you, face to the ground, etc." [and] (Isaiah 60:14), "Bowing before you, shall come the children of those who tormented you." For all will subjugate themselves and bow down to them to receive - through them - the bright light of God, blessed be He, that rests upon them. And see that their pride will be lowered and they will humble themselves below Israel. And they will repent through them to His service, may He be blessed. So, all of the matter of the lulav and its details follow this, as we have written.

Chanukah and Purim: The content of Chanukah and Purim is to bring out the light that shines during those days, according to the refinements that were refined by them: Chanukah is about the priests (Kohanim) overpowering the evil Greeks, who intended to take Israel away from the service of God. But the priests strengthened themselves, and - through them - [the other Jews] came back to the Torah and the [divine] service, especially that of the Menorah according to its practices, about which there were accusers; whereas the priests brought it back to its propriety. And Purim concerns the matter of the salvation of Israel during the Babylonian exile; and the accepting of the Torah again. For they then accepted it again forever, as they, may their memory be blessed, said (Shabbat 88a), "They went back and accepted it at the time of Ahasuerus." And the details of their content are according to the details of the refinement.

The shofar (horn): Whereas the content of the shofar on Rosh Hashanah is [as follows]: Behold the Holy One, blessed be He, judges the whole entire world and renews all of existence with regard to the new cycle - meaning the new year. And see that the courts are arranged and the case is prepared for all of the creation, according to the arrangements of supreme justice, as we wrote in Part II (On the System of Providence 5). And the prosecutor is prepared to prosecute according to people's iniquities. So, see that the Holy One, blessed be He, commanded us to blow the shofar. And its intention is to bring down merciful - and not harsh - direction; and to confuse the prosecutor, so, that he will not prosecute. And note that we have already explained in Part II (On Specific Modes of Prophecy 1) that just like the attribute of strict justice does not allow that good come to people if they have not merited it, so, too is it an axiom of justice that the appropriate and case-specific reward for some actions that people do be that it treat them in their general judgement with mercy and compassion, and not be precise with total exactitude towards them. And it is like the matter which they, may their memory be blessed, said (Rosh Hashanah 17a), "[Regarding] anyone who forgoes his reckonings [with others for injustices done to him, the heavenly court] forgoes [punishment] for all his transgressions." For this is poetic justice - just as he yields, so, will they yield to him. And it comes out that they act with mercy towards him; but this too is from [God's] characteristic of justice. However, this is not the only act for which one is rewarded this way. Rather any act that the Supreme Wisdom decreed appropriate for it to be rewarded this way, will be rewarded this way. And among them is this commandment of blowing the shofar, about which Israel was commanded, so, as to bring down merciful direction [of the world]. So, when they observe it properly, this will be the fruit that they can reap from it. Of course, the specific relationship between the blowing of the shofar and the bringing down of mercy is dependent upon the roots of the direction and its true foundations: The true intention of this is to arouse the patriarchs of the world, to be strengthened by their merit - such as to arouse mercy and appease the attribute of strict justice, enhance the good over the bad, suppress the forces of evil, take away the power of the prosecutors and intend that the Master, blessed be He, use His pre-eminence to act with the rule of His Unity, so, as to forego transgression. And all of this [happens] through this commandment when it is combined with Israel's proper repentance. And all the details of this matter are according to the details of this refinement with its attributes.

Yom Kippur: However, the content of Yom Kippur is [as follows]: Behold the Master, blessed be He, prepared a day for Israel on which repentance would be easily accepted and iniquities readily erased - meaning to rectify all of the corruptions that were done by them, remove all of the darkness that was strengthened by them and to bring back the penitents to the level of holiness and closeness to Him, may He blessed, from which they had become distanced through their sins. And see that on this day, a light shine that has the power to fulfill this whole matter. However, it is a light that, in order to be received, requires that Israel observe that which they were commanded for this day - and especially the matter of affliction (fasting, etc.), through which they are greatly removed from physicality and partially elevated to the character of angels. And all of the rest of the details of the things are according to the details of the refinement.

The reading of the Torah: And behold you need to know that among the great refinements arranged by the prophets for Israel is the matter of Torah readings. And this includes two aspects: The first is reading the Torah scroll in order - to its completion - and repeating the cycle in this way. And the second is the reading of special sections for special times. And this is because the scroll of the Torah is surely the sum of that which He, may He be blessed, gave over to us, for us to meditate upon it. For though this, His emanation is brought down to us, as we have written in Part I (On Human Responsibility 9) and in this part as well, in Chapter 2 (On Torah Study 2). But behold that to receive this emanation regularly, they ordained that we should go over it regularly, in order, in our congregations. And this is besides the private meditation that is appropriate for each and every one individually. And behold that through this regular reading, this holy light is constantly within us. But on the special days, it is also, appropriate that we read the sections that relate to their content, and strengthen the emanation of these days through the power of the Torah - which is the strongest power that we have.

On Blessings

But conditional service is comprised of events that happen to people during all the days of their lives - according to their situation in this world - concerning their foods, their clothes, their other human needs and their societal affairs. And the general principle upon which all of them are based is that which we have explained in previous sections: That is that you do not have any matter in the world at all - constant or conditional - in any entity, that is not established and designed according to what needs to exist according to the true purpose of creation that we mentioned above. For all of these details are necessary to achieve it with perfection -

each one according to the limits that have truly been placed upon it. However, the need for all of the details and their forms follows from the [various] parts of existence, their gradation and the influences upon them - according to their types and their levels, as we have written above. And note that we were commanded commandments about all of these matters - according to their contents - to hold the things towards good, and not towards evil. For when these acts are held within these limits, their content will be towards the good; and that which will follow from, and be caused by, them will be good and refined. But if they are not kept [within their limits], these acts will end up towards evil. Then - through them - impurity, pollution and great darkness will spread; the supreme emanation will be lacking; and [God's] hiddenness will increase. Then all of the bad effects that we mentioned will follow. It is all due to this matter that is not contained within its limits and its [appropriate] relationship with man, with that which surrounds it and with the general mechanism of the entities moving in their processes in order to be perfectly fixed - as we have written above.

Regarding blessings over pleasure: And behold that the matter of blessings that they, may their memory be blessed, ordained - upon all the matters of the world and its pleasures - is based upon this approach. And the root of all of them is the Grace after the Meals, about which we were commanded in the Torah. And this matter results from that which we have surely already explained - that all things in existence and designed by nature, are surely all designed towards the general purpose, which is all of existence reaching perfection. And their portion in this is according to the level of their true existence. Yet man - who is pulled after the properties of his nature, and acts according to that which is designed in him - must always have his Creator's service in mind; as well as [awareness] that what comes out of these actions be a function and aid to the fulfillment of this purpose - whatever the path [towards it] might be - according to how the things were truly arranged. The explanation of this is that there will be some things that already serve this [purpose] right away; yet there will be other things that will serve other functions until - after a long process of many things, one following another - they come to it. However, regardless of the stage the things are in, it is only fit to take them, with this intent of what comes from them - even if it is [only] after ten stages that help reach the purpose - and not with any other intent; meaning intents of desires and inclination towards the physical, towards extra luxuries. And he should guard all of them with the limits that the divine Torah legislated for them. And then they will truly be helping this thing and will be considered preconditions of the [divine] service. So, behold that the Torah taught us that after we have enjoyed our food and drink, we should give thanks in front of Him, may He be blessed, bless His name and bring the thing back to its true function, which is to aid the general purpose, as we mentioned. [In this way], it comes out that His glory, may He be blessed, is enhanced - in that His will is done and his counsel fulfilled. And this is the general content of the Grace after the Meals and, likewise, of the other blessings of enjoyment (over food) after enjoyment. However, to enhance this matter, they, may their memory be blessed, added the ordinance of blessings before enjoyment. And that is that even before a man uses something from the world, he should mention His name, may He be blessed, over it, bless Him, and have in mind that this good thing came to him from [God]. And he should intend that this good is not just something physical and a material enjoyment; but rather that it is something prepared by Him, may He be blessed, for the true function of the good that will come out of it, as we have written. And by having the matter precede the act, that act will remain completely [directed] towards good, and not towards evil. And man will be refined by it and raised; and not corrupted nor lowered, as we have written.

Regarding blessings over the commandments: However, the Sages also, ordained these blessings for us with the performance of commandments, for the sake of endearing the commandment - to thank Him, may He be blessed, for wanting us and giving us such great refinements as these. And it comes out that through this, the act is more elevated, such that man is helped by Him, may He be blessed. For this is the rule: According to people's arousal towards Him, may He be blessed, so, is the measure of help that He helps them - whether a little or a great deal - in any act whatsoever, according to what it is. And happy is the one who trusts in God.

Finished and completed

praise to God, Creator of the world.

Derech Part Four **Hashem**

www.ingramcontent.com/pod-product-compliance
Lightning Source LLC
Chambersburg PA
CBHW070140080526
44586CB00015B/1771